Visible Jesus

Visible Jesus

LIVING EVERY DAY TO MAKE HIM
KNOWN

Brian Edwards

CrossLink Publishing
CASTLE ROCK, CO

Edwards/CrossLink Publishing
558 E. Castle Pines Pkwy, STE B4117
Castle Rock, CO 80108
www.crosslinkpublishing.com

Ordering Information:
Quantity sales. Special discounts are available on quantity pur-
chases by corporations, associations, and others. For details,
contact the "Special Sales Department" at the address above.

Visible Jesus/ Brian Edwards —1st ed.
ISBN 978-1-63357-133-4

Library of Congress Control Number: 2017961479

The definition of cliché is: a trite phrase or expression, something that has become overly familiar or common place.

Unfortunately, this definition not only describes a word, but it also describes the lives of many Christians who have become experts on how to look, act, and sound. The sad thing is in most cases, it is only skin deep. Too many Christians are a living cliché with no real substance or genuine desire to imitate the one they profess to love and follow.

Visible Jesus goes into great detail to give believers vital information about truly knowing and following Jesus. It is challenging and thought-provoking. It lovingly forces experienced Christians to examine whether or not they are pursuing Jesus, or expertly living as a religious cliché.

Malcolm Carter, Lead Pastor of Temple Baptist Church, Cullman, Alabama.

Visible Jesus is a masterpiece of commonsense biblical teaching in a world gone astray. Many today have mastered the art of religion, but few truly emulate the risen Christ. This book will truly challenge your walk with God, encourage you to review your life, and answer the question, "When people see me, do they see Jesus?" I highly recommend this important work.

Dr. Michael T. George, best-selling author of *My Story of America, 3:16 The Story Of God and Author Of Liberty*

We are living in a world crying out for help, and the silence of Christianity is deafening. Pastor Brian Edwards does a masterful job showing that it is not the world that is getting darker, but it is the lack of light from those who make up the Church. *Visible Jesus* awakens the Christian to the need to share the Gospel, not just with the nations, but with our neighbors as well.

Dr. Rodney Agan, Founder of Connexus Group

In his book *Visible Jesus*, Brian Edwards reminds us that if the world is going to change, it will be because of Jesus. By using scripture, along with personal stories, in a conversational way, Brian engages the reader, and calls him or her to come out of the shadows and live to make Jesus visible by every means possible.

Ray Carroll, Founder of Fallen Pastors Ministries

My friend Brian Edwards has written a book that every pastor and every Christian should read and take to heart. He identifies a major problem in contemporary Christianity—we are not making Jesus visible to the culture around us—and he is honest enough not to deny his own culpability. He does provide insight and motivation for changing that, however.

As I was finishing reading *Visible Jesus* just now, I had an overwhelming desire to immediately get up, go outside, and find someone to talk to about Jesus. I think you'll have the same reaction.

Brian is a good pastor, a fine preacher, and now I see that he is an excellent writer too!

Don Davidson, Senior Pastor of First Baptist Alexandria, Virginia

Brian has strategically forced us to look around at the absence of Jesus in our culture, but then he unexpectedly compels all to acknowledge His absence within us. This book will expose the emptiness in you and then lead you to seek only the Jesus centered life. A timely solution to an empty existence!

Pastor Jon Bowman, Senior Pastor of Peace Haven Baptist Church

Not only has Brian Edwards lived a life that makes Jesus visible, he now shows us through this new book, Visible Jesus, practical ways we too can make Jesus visible in our own daily lives. This is a must read for any Jesus follower who wants to make Jesus known to the people around them.

Mark Neal, Lead Pastor, Hamilton Hills Church, Fishers, Indiana

Dedication

No one has influenced me more than you. No one has taught me to love God and His word more than you. No one else knew me as a rebellious teenage boy, and repeatedly reminded me that God had great plans for my life. Hundreds of people have called you pastor, thousands have called you preacher, but I am one of only three who has the privilege of calling you Daddy.

Dedication

Contents

Preface

In no way do I feel worthy to write a book. Reading behind great pastors and authors makes me fully aware of all of my limitations and fully aware of the amazing resources readily available to Christians.

There has never been a time in my life when the voice of my insecurity hasn't been whispering words of self-doubt in my ear, and to be completely honest, too often I have listened to that voice. However, this book isn't about my qualifications; it is about a message that has consumed me. In Acts 4:20, the Holy Spirit filled Peter with a supernatural boldness. A few chapters earlier he followed Jesus afar off, denied that he was a disciple, and even went into hiding, but in Acts 4:20 he exclaimed, "for we cannot but speak of what we have seen and heard." Being silent was not an option.

That's how I feel about the words written on these pages. God has made this truth so big in my heart that I can't keep it to myself. I have to speak out about what I have seen and heard. So this book called *Visible Jesus* isn't about me, but it is ultimately about a truth that has consumed me, and I've written every word believing Jesus' promise in 2 Corinthians 12:9, that His power is made perfect in our weakness.

Truly He is greater than any of our human limitations, and He works beyond our weaknesses to accomplish His great purposes. I have tried to be faithful to write what He has placed on my heart, and I pray He will use this book to inspire you to make Jesus visible.

Acknowledgments

"I thank my God in all of my remembrance of you."
(Philippians 1:3)

After twenty-eight years of marriage, I am still discovering the enormous worth and value of my wife, Denise. She has graciously fulfilled a role that she never dreamed of having, and I couldn't imagine my life in ministry without her. Hearing her say the words, "Brian, I believe God is really going to use this book," encouraged me more than I could ever express.

The staff of Hope Church is beyond capable. I am grateful that they were willing to spur me on to the good work of writing this book, and were willing to make sure I had the time. I am forever grateful to serve God alongside each of them.

I appreciate Taylor McKinnis, Nathan Cravatt, and Jesse Young for reading the book over and over again and for allowing me to read to them over the phone and ask, "How does that sound?" They were great sounding boards, and constant encouragers.

Thank you to each of the men who were willing to take time out of their busy schedules to read *Visible Jesus* for the purpose of writing an endorsement. Each one of them are special to me, and the fact they read my unedited book and still endorsed it says that I'm special to them. I also owe a special thank you to my niece, Lexi Toufas. The hours she invested editing the book were not only a gift to me, but to every person who will read *Visible Jesus*.

CrossLink Publishing, thank you so much for believing in the book and for being willing to give me the amazing opportunity to share it with others. I appreciate that you view publishing as a ministry more than you view it as a business. I am forever grateful.

A special thank you to Alan Dalton Photography for using their expertise and offering it as a gift. Alan is not just a photographer—he is a cherished friend.

Last of all, I want to thank God for each person who has invested in my life through supporting Hope Church and supporting me. God has truly lavished His grace on my life in so many ways that I could never count them all, and each of you have been among His greatest gifts of grace.

Introduction

Over the past few years I have traveled to more cities and states than I have at any other time in my life. I've been from Canada to California, from the southern part of Georgia to the southern part of Alaska, from the coast of Maine to the canyons of Wyoming, and so many other places in between. Since I'm starting to get a little older (very little), I'm noticing that I'm more aware of beautiful scenery and more apt to stop to soak it in. When I was younger, I was always on a mission, but now that I'm getting older, I'm realizing that I'm on a journey. The old saying "stop and smell the roses" means more now than it ever has before.

However, over the past few years, it hasn't been *what I have seen* in different cities and states that has grabbed my attention, but it's been *what I haven't seen*. When I stopped focusing on what I had to do, where I had to go, or what I wanted to see, and I started looking for Jesus, regardless of where I was, I didn't see Him. Crowded streets in the Bible Belt, and busy restaurants in large, liberal metropolitan cities all had one thing in common—Jesus was virtually invisible. The more aware I became of His absence, the more aware I became of my need to make Him visible.

Visible Jesus wasn't birthed in my heart as a result of my success in making Him visible; it was birthed in my heart as a result of the conviction I felt when I realized my failure to make Him visible. Instead of asking myself the question, "Why am I not seeing Jesus?" I started asking, "What am I doing every day to make Him known?" That question has changed my life.

The greatest thing that could ever be said to a Christian would be, "You are a lot like Jesus," but sadly there are very few people living their daily lives to earn that comparison. As a matter of fact, we've gotten so busy with our own lives and our own interest that we rarely even think about making Jesus visible. Seldom do we stop to share Jesus with the people we meet, but that has to change. As Christians, we have to start living with an awareness of our responsibility to make Him known.

We have to see that His identity is being intentionally erased from every aspect of community and culture—even in many churches. Like a teacher erases the blackboard at the end of a class period, the real Jesus of the Bible is being methodically and intentionally removed from the public square right before our eyes. We are witnessing the disappearance of Jesus in our nation, and we are the only ones who can change that. Christians are the only people on the planet who are capable of revealing Jesus to the world. That is our mission.

Mark Driscoll wrote in his book, *A Call to Resurgence,*

> We have been chosen by God to live at this time and in this culture with all its faults and flaws, as part of the church of Jesus Christ with all her faults and flaws, as people with all our

own faults and flaws. Today we have an unprecedented opportunity for mission. Christendom may have died, but in that death there is a real opportunity for a resurgence of biblically faithful, personally humble, evangelistically fruitful, missional Christianity.

People have seen our multimillion-dollar church buildings, they have heard our well-written songs, many of them have encountered our impactful programs, and they still aren't convinced. Could it be because none of those things possess a fraction of the power of the person who is living to make Jesus visible? Steeples and sanctuaries, music and mid-week services, pews and programs will never be as effective as one Christian who lives to make Jesus visible. Will you be that Christian?

"Have you no wish for others to be saved? Then you're not saved yourself, be sure of that!"

Charles Haddon Spurgeon

CHAPTER 1

DO WE REALIZE
THE PROBLEM?

A ll it takes is a glance—just one quick glance across the landscape of our culture—to notice the absence of Jesus. It's true. If you mentally reenact your day, carefully looking for His presence in every nook and cranny, you will notice just how invisible He is in the spaces that you occupy. Look down the hallway of your local school or across the classroom at the university...do you see Him? Look around your office, or across the aisle at the factory where you work, or in the cubicle next to yours...is He there? Do you see Him on television or hear Him in the lyrics of popular music? The answer is no, isn't it? He really isn't visible in any of those places. Even more troubling is the internal unrest that occurs when you admit that He isn't visible in the sanctuary of your church or the family room of your home.

Most of the time we live completely unaware of His absence because we fail to intentionally look for Him. He is like a lost object; we don't know it's missing until we try to find it, and it's when we are unable to find it that we realize it's lost. All of us have experienced that, haven't we? Suddenly needing that one, important receipt to complete our tax return, or needing the screwdriver with the black and yellow handle to make a repair, or needing an ink pen to quickly write down a phone number, but when we look where we're confident we left it, it's not there. That is when the thing we hadn't thought about in months until moments earlier becomes the most urgent thing in our lives. Realizing something is lost automatically creates a certain amount of desperation. Most people even make statements like, "I have to find that _____."

Jesus shared a parable in Luke 15:8–10 about a widow who lost a coin. She had ten, which meant after losing one, she still had nine left, but in Jesus' parable, the one that was lost captivated her attention. Jesus carefully worded the parable to express how urgently she searched for the single coin she had lost. He asked, "Doesn't she light a lamp, sweep the house, and search carefully until she finds it?" Jesus was making the point to His audience of crooked tax collectors and sinners that when something is lost, there is both urgency to find it, and celebration when you finally do. We all know the tension that exists when we lose something and the relief that is felt when we find it. Whether it's our keys, the television remote, or our debit card, losing something important brings everything to a screeching halt until it's found.

When I was a younger pastor, I had a habit of jotting down sermon ideas on any piece of paper I could find. Back then I thought every sermon idea was a great idea. Who knew which one of those ideas might change the world? My cell phone didn't have an app that stored notes, and a laptop computer was way too expensive for a struggling church planter, so small scrap pieces of paper were an efficient, but not effective means of sermon preparation. During those days, I was working a full-time, third-shift job as well as planting the church. There was barely any time to study, and that made those pieces of paper extremely important to me. Truth be told, they had no value at all, but to me they were golden. Trust me, I needed every one of those ideas just to survive.

One week had been especially busy. Not only had I worked third-shift for seven consecutive days, but my days had also been filled with visiting the sick, caring for the grieving and fulfilling my responsibilities around our house. In all honesty, I hadn't had time to study; if I had tried, my face would have been buried in the Bible and drool would have ruined the pages. Sitting down meant falling asleep. I'll never forget driving the forklift at Times Fiber Corporation, wondering what in the world I was going to preach. To answer that question, I needed to put my hands on the piece of paper that contained my latest sermon ideas. "Honey, have you seen the piece of paper that had my sermons written on it?" I called out to my wife, Denise. "It's not where I left it, and you're the one who cleaned up." Of course she responded with, "No, I haven't seen it." I knew that was what she was going to say, but it was not what I wanted to hear. I had to have that piece of paper, and I had to have it immediately.

Frantically, I started opening every drawer, looking through every closet and under every cushion. I knew it had to be in our house somewhere, and I was going to find it, or else. For the next few hours, I searched for that one little scrap piece of paper. I didn't stop to think of all of the time I was wasting. It didn't cross my mind to invest that time digging into God's word in order to find a truth to share with His church. I was too busy digging through drawers and closets. Something important was lost, and that was all I could think about at that moment.

Realizing something is lost creates a certain amount of desperation. Searching for a lost item, object, or person can easily become an obsession, but why doesn't that apply to Jesus?

In Luke 2:43, Joseph and Mary didn't realize they had left Jesus in Jerusalem. The Passover feast had ended, and the sixty-four-mile journey back to Nazareth was underway. They assumed Jesus was with them. Surely, He was somewhere in the crowd. He wasn't visible, they couldn't see Him, but they "supposed" He was there, the Bible says. It wasn't until they realized His absence that they started searching. Imagine them running from person to person, frantically asking, "Have you seen Jesus?" Imagine them nervously scanning the crowd, hoping they had just overlooked Him. Picture Mary in tears, asking Joseph, "Where could He be?" They would have been desperate to find Him once they realized His absence, but how much better would it have been if they hadn't been so careless? How much better would it have been for them to be so aware of His presence that they were immediately aware of His absence?

Several years ago, my little girl came running into the bedroom and said, "Daddy, Daddy, guess what I can do?" I responded, "What can you do, darling?" She excitedly said, "I can quote John 3:16...do you want to hear me?" "You better believe I do," I said in an excited tone of voice. A big smile came across her face as she stood up big and tall to quote John 3:16 for me. I could tell by her expression that she couldn't possibly be any more serious about the opportunity to impress her daddy. I can still hear her now, her cute mispronunciations and the pitch of her voice ringing out about two octaves higher than usual. She started out perfectly, "for God so loved the world, that He gave," but it was her mistake in the next phrase that left me heartbroken and in tears. She didn't quote what was in the Bible, but she quoted what she thought she had heard. Instead of saying, "that He gave His only begotten Son," she said, "that He gave His only forgotten Son."

That isn't what we see when we read John 3:16, but that is what we see when we look around us. We know Jesus is invisible in our culture, we know His absence is obvious, and yet we no longer look for Him or expect people to look for Him in us. We intellectually agree that people should see Him in us, but any conviction associated with that intellectual acknowledgment usually gets stored away, and we plan to do better someday. Rarely do we conform our lives to accommodate the conviction we feel. Yes, Jesus needs to be visible...no, we're not willing to do whatever we need to do, and we're not willing to change whatever we need to change to make Him visible in our lives. We would rather continue living in spiritual lethargy. Demolishing the familiarity and security of our comfort zones is too difficult. We would rather turn a blind eye than be honest about the absence of Jesus around us and in us.

We are seeing the effects of a culture without Jesus. A culture where Christianity is just that—cultural. Racism, sexual hedonism, atheism, terrorism, materialism, secularism, and amoralism are all symptoms of a nation that removes Jesus from the public square.

We all know that the world around us is getting worse, and there is a growing mountain of evidence that proves our continual digression—it's happening rapidly! Increased violence, division, and hatred are becoming increasingly common. Mass shootings like the one in Las Vegas, Nevada, or racial clashes like the one in Charlottesville, Virginia, all-too-often dominate the twenty-four-hour news cycle. Words that were once virtually unknown are now a part of our common language; sex trafficking, terrorism, cyber crime, Internet pornography, political correctness, substance abuse, and gender fluidity have all forced their way into our conversations. Behaviors and lifestyles that were once unacceptable even among non-Christians have exited the shadows and are now being paraded on the big stage of mainstream culture.

With every change we seem to take another step farther away from Jesus and deeper into despair. The voice and the presence of culture grows louder and bolder while the voice of the church and the Christian grows quieter and more timid. The result of our national disobedience and spiritual unconcern is that the presence of Jesus is increasingly obscured. The artillery of our negative world advances more aggressively, constantly encroaching on all that is spiritual, right, pure, and wholesome. That is why people are echoing the sentiment that something needs to be done! Something needs to happen to reverse the downward spiral of our nation.

Some in the Christian community think our response to the severe cultural problems of our nation should be to isolate ourselves. They live as if they believe Christians need to disappear into church buildings, private fellowships, and homes. Verses are taken out of context and used to advance the message, be more distant, more secluded. Like doomsday preppers, they believe we should all retreat to the bomb shelters of our religious safe places, but we should know that isn't biblical Christianity. We should know better than to think there is any hope at all in isolation or distance. The dark corridors of our culture will never be illuminated by the "Christians" who retreat into hiding, or adopt a more militant attitude toward our broken world. Those who spew out blanketing insults and demonstrate divisive behavior will never be a beacon of hope. Representing Jesus in that way is not the answer, and it will never be the answer. It is the opposite of Christianity. The desperate need of a culture that is lost and wandering is to see Jesus through people who love Him, and them. The world around us has an immeasurable need to see Jesus on display in the everyday lives of Christians everywhere. Our culture desperately needs to encounter believers who are living, moving, walking, talking billboards displaying the love and life of Jesus. That's what the world needs to see most—people who are consumed with making Jesus visible.

Every problem has a source, and the disappearance of Jesus in our culture is no different. The issue is correctly identifying the source, and then being willing to do whatever is necessary to solve the problem. I saw the perfect example of this truth on one of my favorite television shows several months ago. Everyone who knows me knows that I love all things Alaska. Whether it's Marty battling the elements in the Alaskan wilderness on

Mountain Men, or Otto, Ivan and Atz herding cattle at the head of the bay on *Alaska The Last Frontier*, or Todd Hoffman and Parker Schnabel digging for gold on *Gold Rush Alaska*, I just love all of those shows. So much so that in 2016, I stood by the sign that read "Welcome to Homer Alaska" and sang the theme song of one of my favorite programs that is filmed there.

One weekly series I enjoy watching on National Geographic is called *Port Protection*. The show chronicles the struggles of the small group of people who live in a remote fishing village, and primarily depend on Alaska's natural resources. Often an hour-long episode will be dedicated to a few of the residents coming together to address a shared problem, and it was during one of those problem-solving episodes that I saw a physical picture of a spiritual issue. The people of Port Protection were experiencing a water crisis. Their freshwater supply had been diminished to nothing more than a trickle, and the problem had to be solved. In remote Alaska, there are no city-maintained water systems or well-drilling companies. Therefore, the primary source of fresh water is streams and springs. In Port Protection, the people depend on a small polyvinyl chloride pipe that runs down the side of the mountain bringing them water from a cold spring. The system is incredibly simple, so the lack of water pointed to either a blockage or a severe leak. However, the problem couldn't be fully corrected until it was first identified.

Two of Port Protection's handymen gathered a few tools and started the slow process of inspecting the water line. Along the way they found a few leaks and a few distressed areas, but nothing severe enough to cut off the water supply. Knowing they hadn't yet found the problem forced them to continue their search. One step at a time, they climbed the mountain side, surveying the water line, until they finally reached the cold-water spring, and once they did, they realized the problem. The small pond at the mouth of the spring was so filled with sediment that the pipe that delivered their water was clogged. This important discovery allowed them to fix the problem, but they had to first be willing to reach the source. In the same way the residents of Port Protection had to deal with the disappearance of freshwater in their community, Christians have to be willing to deal with the disappearance of Jesus in our communities, and the problem has a source.

For too long, Christians have been blaming everyone and everything for the disappearance of Jesus in our nation. Christians have blamed people like Madalyn O'Hair, Christopher Hitchens and Richard Dawkins. Christians have blamed national sins like abortion, gay marriage, and pornography. Certain parts of the Christian community have blamed music, movies, and television. Some Christians have even blamed public education, liberal universities, and political agendas. The list of people and things being held accountable for the lack of Jesus' visibility in our culture seems to be endless. The problem with the constant finger-pointing that has taken place is that it fails to correctly identify the problem. It's true we have committed national sins that are absolutely opposed to Jesus' work and His word. It's also true that both our entertainment industry and our educational system have grown increasingly secular and willing to discard traditional values, but it is still true that none of them are to blame.

They aren't to blame because they were never responsible for making Jesus visible. That task was never given
to Washington, D.C., or any political party. Schools and
universities were never sent out by Jesus to saturate the
world with His presence. Music and movies can be used
as great tools in a media-driven world, but they were never employed by Jesus to make disciples. The responsibility of making Jesus visible in every culture and to every
generation has always belonged to Christians. That means
Christians are always to blame when the identity of Jesus
diminishes around them. It's not a cultural problem, but a
church problem. The problem is not at the bottom of the
mountain, in "the world," but rather at the mouth of the
spring, in the church. Jesus declared Himself to be "living water" in John 4:10, but He isn't flowing through us
into our communities, or through us into our schools, or
through us into our workplaces, and if we're honest we
will admit that it is because of all of the sediment that's
clogging our lives.

In Matthew 7:3–4, Jesus asked the question, "Why do
you see the speck that is in your brother's eye, but do
not notice the log that is in your own eye? Or how can
you say to your brother, let me take the speck out of your
eye, when there is a log in your own eye?" Jesus' questions were straightforward. He was asking His disciples,
how are you going to deal with someone else's problem
until you first deal with your own? He then followed His
questions with a strong statement in Matthew 7:5: "You
hypocrite, first take the log out of your own eye...." In
other words, deal with your own problem first. That's
what Jesus instructed His disciples to do, but that's not
what we're doing.

For so long Christians have avoided dealing with our own failures by looking outward rather than inward. We've scolded the world for acting like the world, but very seldom have we scolded ourselves for our failure to act like Christians. Jesus' identity and influence have slowly been erased from our culture and we've blamed the symptoms rather than the problem, but if the church could stand shoulder-to-shoulder and peer into an enormous full-length mirror, then we would finally be looking at the real problem. It's not the nonbelievers fault that we look so much like them that we're failing to look like Him. We are the source of the problem.

R. Albert Mohler Jr. wrote in his powerful book, *The Disappearance of God*, "Secularization, the process by which society severs its ties to a religious worldview, is now pressed to the limits by ideological secularists bent on removing all vestiges of the Judeo-Christian heritage from the nation's culture." That is exactly what's happening around us, but that shouldn't be what is happening in us. The ideological secularist may be given the power to remove Jesus from the culture, but they must never be given the power to remove Jesus from the mouths and the lives of Christians. The world is never going to make Jesus known, but that doesn't give Christians an excuse not to. Our conviction to make Him known has to be stronger than the culture's opposition. Our commitment to display Jesus in our daily lives has to be stronger than culture's desire to remove Him from the public eye. Our resolve as individuals needs to be that Jesus has to be made visible, and it depends on each one of us.

REFLECT

1. What are some lifestyle changes you could make that would increase Jesus' visibility in your life?

2. How does Luke 2:43 parallel with your home and life?

3. What are some ways you could help move Christianity from a church sanctuary into your community?

4. If you thoroughly examined your own life would you find blame or repentance?

5. How can you apply Matthew 7:3–4 in a way that increases Jesus being visible in your life?

"In a word, the evangelistic message is the gospel of Christ, and Him crucified, the message of man's sin and God's grace, of human guilt and divine forgiveness, of new birth and new life through the Holy Spirit."

J.I. Packer

CHAPTER 2

YOU HAVE TO KNOW JESUS TO MAKE HIM VISIBLE

Our middle daughter, Sydney, has this unique ability to impersonate people. It's a talent she's always had as far back as we can remember. Even as a little girl she would mimic people in our family or reenact the way I had preached a sermon. One of my favorite memories of her impersonating other people happened when she was only about five years old. I picked her up from my parents one Sunday afternoon, and as we were making the drive home, I kept hearing her shout from the back seat as loudly as she could, "Amen!" She would hold the growl for a few seconds in the beginning and then slowly belt it out at full force. Finally, I asked her, "Sydney, what are you doing?" She said, "I'm saying amen like the people at Papa's church." "You're doing what?" I responded. She said, "That's what the people do at Papa's church after the songs, and while Papa is preaching, they shout out Aaaa-mayan (Amen)." Needless to say, I laughed so hard that I almost had to pull off of the road and park the car until I regained my composure.

Her impersonations have always made us laugh. Most of the time at someone else's expense, but since we're a family of five with a limited budget, we've always welcomed the free entertainment. That has always been her goal, after all, to entertain us, but just because her "copycatting" is funny and entertaining, that doesn't change the fact that there is a certain amount of science behind her hilarious impersonations. Observing, memorizing, and replicating are all a part of the end result. She notices voice inflections, accents, repetitions, mannerisms, facial expressions, even twitches and ticks. She does it so well that no one ever asks her who she is pretending to be. The usual reaction is, "Oh my gosh! That is just like them! How did you even notice them saying that? How did you notice them doing that?" The answer is obvious: she has been around that person long enough to observe him or her, and through observation, she has learned his or her behaviors. Over time, she has listened to the person talk, watched his or her movements, and cataloged the things he or she repeatedly says or does.

Even with her talent to impersonate other people, it would be impossible for her to accurately impersonate someone she has never seen or heard. Just because it's entertaining doesn't mean that she hasn't invested the time and energy required to reproduce someone's characteristics. After all, that's what impersonating requires. Celebrity impersonator Rufus Stone said, "The thing is, that if you don't believe that you are an old man, or a woman, or a tramp, then how can you expect anyone else to believe you? Looking the part is just the surface; being the part is the true disguise."

Successful impersonators must be able to imitate and copy the behaviors and actions of other people. By definition, impersonating demands that you study another person thoroughly enough to reproduce them in yourself. Maybe that's why so few Christians are actually portraying who Jesus is, to a world that doesn't know Him. Maybe that's why our impersonation of Him remains non-existent. Maybe that is the culprit that has led to the absence of His identity in our culture. The problem is not that the characteristics of Jesus have decreased in effectiveness, or that the life and love of Jesus have lost their power to change the environment around us. The problem is, Christians aren't intentionally investing the time and energy required to know who Jesus truly is. We can't talk like Him if we aren't familiar with His words, and we can't walk like Him if we haven't retraced His steps. We can't display Him in our lives if we haven't submersed ourselves in His life.

That is the basis of being a disciple of Jesus—submersing yourself in His life, His words, and His characteristics. Disciples of Jesus follow Jesus for the purpose of imitating Him. That's what disciples do—they imitate their leader. That's what sets a true disciple apart. A disciple strives to take on the identity of Jesus. True followers of Jesus never pursue Him for what they can get from Him; true followers follow, knowing that Jesus is the ultimate reward. That's what we see even in Jesus' initial call to discipleship in Matthew 4:20. While walking on the shoreline of Galilee, Jesus called out to a few young fishermen, "follow me." That was the extent of His invitation. It wasn't "follow me and I will give you wealth," or "follow me and will give you good health," or "follow me and I will provide you with a more comfortable life." He didn't promise to give the young men who followed Him anything other than Himself. The call would have sounded a lot like, "follow me so that you can follow me," and yet the Bible says, they immediately forsook their nets, their boats, their livelihoods, and they followed Jesus. They followed Him so their lives could be devoted to following Him. That was the life of the disciples throughout the gospels: pursuing Jesus, listening to Jesus, serving with Jesus, and obeying Jesus. That was their whole life. An ongoing, daily study of Jesus in real situations and circumstances.

There was no classroom, but that didn't mean that Jesus wasn't teaching. Class was definitely in session, and He was teaching them moment by moment. He was teaching them about faith when He placed them in a storm during the darkest part of the night. He was teaching them about divine sufficiency when He took five loaves and two fish and fed the multitude. He was teaching them about forgiveness when He saved the life of an adulteress by convincing an angry mob to consider their own sinful condition. He was teaching them about the gospel when He gathered them around a table and likened His body to the broken bread and His blood to the wine. Every moment with Jesus was a learning experience; every action was an example for them to follow. Jesus was pouring Himself into the disciples so that even in His absence the world would still encounter His presence. Jesus' final commission to them was, do what you've seen me do—make disciples. Make me known to the world by impersonating me in the world.

He had every right to ask them to do that since He was their Rabbi. Their life's mission was to be exactly like Him. Their days were spent studying His every move and hearing His every word. The disciples knew they were expected to intentionally shed their own identities in order to take on the identity of their teacher. The September 2005 issue of the endearing little devotional, *Our Daily Bread* said this:

> The disciple's calling, as described in early Jewish writings about basic ethics, was to, 'cover himself in the dust of [the rabbi's] feet,' drinking in his every word. He followed the rabbi so closely that he would 'walk in his dust.' In doing so, he became like the rabbi, his master.

If the disciples desired to be like Jesus, they all knew that distance mattered. A disciple couldn't be like his master apart from closeness. Intimate knowledge could only be gained by closely following, not for minutes, or moments, or hours. Not periodically or for short walks, but consistently, day after day, step after step, mile after mile. That was, and still is today, the only way. We can't accurately impersonate Jesus without living in a close relationship with Him.

Distance always diminishes influence, and distance in the life of a disciple always leads to failure. Peter was most unlike Jesus the night he followed afar off. Denying and cursing were symptoms of the distance he had created between him and Jesus. He would have never talked like that had he been by Jesus' side, but Jesus wasn't by the fire. Peter couldn't see Him or hear Him, and that certainly contributed to his heartbreaking failure. His behavior, to some degree, was the result of his proximity, and he didn't preach with power on the day of Pentecost until his closeness with Jesus was restored. Peter had to have an intimate conversation with Jesus first. He needed to be called to repentance. He had to sit by another fireside and be questioned about the depth of his love.

The last time Peter was by a fireside, he denied that he knew Jesus, but as he sat by the fireside, only inches away from Jesus, his confession was, "Lord you know everything, you know that I love you." It wasn't until after that conversation that he looked like a disciple of Jesus again. Peter had to walk away from those intense moments with Jesus, understanding that constant closeness with Jesus was necessary for a disciple. He couldn't walk beyond the dust cloud created by Jesus' feet without resembling who he used to be before he was called to follow. He had to live out the words of the old hymn that we used to sing in church, "I need Thee, oh I need Thee, every hour I need Thee."

What an incredible lesson for all of us. If only we would realize that our "seen" failures are almost always the result of the "unseen" distance between the Lord and us. If only we would realize that the distance is not the result of our sin, but rather that our sin is the result of the distance (James 1:14). We can't even live the basic Christian life effectively if there is any distance at all between us and Him. Everything falls apart. That's why we must have a driving passion to be covered by the dust from Jesus' feet. Close should always give way to closer.

We should never want to know or try to experience how far we can wander away from Him and still resemble a Christian. Our heart's desire should always be to experience the indescribable joy that results from increased closeness, and our hearts should break the moment we feel the least bit of separation. Any space between Him and us should be too far.

John Piper wrote this prayer in his book *Seeing and Savoring Jesus Christ*, "And we must thank you because you have made us taste and see the glory of Jesus Christ, your son. Oh, to know Him! Father, we long to know Him."

That should be the prayer we pray over and over again. He should be our greatest affection, and our pursuit of knowing Him more should never wane or decrease in intensity. Our desire to know Him, for the purpose of impersonating Him, should govern the way we live. It should determine what we live for, and we must be unwilling to pursue anything that creates distance between us and Him. Regardless of the value of the object or the pleasure found in the experience, it is nothing when compared to knowing Him. "Oh, to know Him! Oh, to know Him! Oh, to know Him!" That should be our continual refrain.

Just imagine how our lives would change if we were as passionate about following Jesus as Ruth was about following Naomi (Ruth 1:16–17). Her heart's cry was clearly heard in her plea to Naomi, "Do not urge me to leave you or to return from following you. For where you go I will go, and where you lodge I will lodge. Your people shall be my people, and your God my God. Where you die I will die, and there will I be buried. May the Lord do so to me and more also if anything but death parts me from you."

That was Ruth's request: Please don't make me walk away. Her resolve proved that nothing meant more to her than being close to Naomi. Ruth didn't know where following her mother-in-law would lead, she didn't know what it would cost, she didn't know what it would require, but Ruth did know that she wanted to follow her regardless. Ruth was willing to abandon everything. Nothing in her life had any value when compared to following in Naomi's footsteps. Her confession was, I'm willing to lose my life, my family, my religion, my dreams, my everything, if that is the cost of following after you.

I read that, and I wonder how our lives would change if we were that passionate about following Jesus. If we were willing to follow that earnestly after Him, how much more evident would He be in our lives? How much would we change, and how much would the world around us change if we were "dusty disciples?"

I fully believe it would change more in us and around us if we lived our daily lives so close to Jesus that we truly knew Him. Our impact on a desperate world would increase exponentially if we spent more time in His presence. That's what the scripture shows us. The disciples knew Jesus more intimately in John 21 when they had breakfast with Him than they did in Matthew 4:19 when they first heard His voice as He spoke the words "follow me." They didn't know Him better because they listened to skilled teachers teaching about Him. They knew Him better because they had walked with Him; they had eaten with Him; they had cried with Him; they had weathered storms with Him. Their proximity had developed their intimacy. There was no substitute for closeness. There is still no substitute for closeness. We can't know Jesus apart from following Him. We must embrace the words of the old hymn, "Wherever He leads, I'll go."

When I was a little boy, my family lived in the foothills of the Blue Ridge Mountains in a tiny community called Ararat, Virginia. There was one store, one restaurant, one fire department, one church, and not much else. I can still remember my Dad turning beside the Blue Ridge Elementary School onto the narrow, winding road that led to our small, A-frame house. I loved those years. There were so many beautiful things about living there. I loved that my bedroom was across the hallway from my parent's bedroom. I loved the big, brick fireplace in the family room. I loved our community and the people who frequently stopped by to visit.

I also loved being surrounded by beautiful mountains. The views were magnificent during every season, but none of that excited me nearly as much as the memorable winter snows. To a little boy, each one seemed like the biggest one ever. I'm sure they were not, but when you're five to eight years old, perception is reality, and I loved thinking "this is the biggest snow ever." That was exactly the kind of snow I woke up to the day my dad invited me to walk down to the dog kennel with him. Of course, my answer was yes! Walking down to the kennel gave me a chance to go out in the snow, but it also meant that I would be close to my daddy. For me, that was a win-win. The only negative was my mom bundling me up like I was going to trek across the arctic circle. She put a stocking cap on my head, big, white socks on my hands, and layers and layers of clothes from my neck to my ankles. Last but not least, she covered everything with the heaviest coat I owned.

Finally, after what seemed like hours of getting dressed, my daddy said the words I had been waiting to hear: "Come on Brian, let's go!" And with those words, that's what he did—he went. Like a man on a mission, he walked across our snow-covered yard in full stride. He was walking so intently that he made it over the hill before he thought to look back and see where I was. He was so focused on getting to the dog kennel that he didn't realize I wasn't able to keep up in the knee-deep snow. So, he turned, stood still, and waited for me to catch up. What he saw as I walked over the knoll of the hill made a permanent impression on his heart. He saw me, stretching my legs just as far apart as I possibly could, in an attempt to walk in his footprints. I was trying with all of my might to step where he had stepped and walk where he had walked. I wanted nothing more than to follow in the footsteps of the one I admired most. At that time, I was just a little boy trying to duplicate the steps of his daddy, but looking back now, I realize that what happened that day was a parable moment. A moment that now profoundly impacts the way I view being a disciple of Jesus.

What happened that day has given me a visual image of walking in Jesus' footsteps. The only way I can be like Him is if I walk in His steps, and the only way I can walk in His steps is if I know the way He walked. He did leave behind footprints, but I have to be close enough to Him to see those footprints. For me, that is what it means to be a disciple. We spend our lives following Him for the purpose of impersonating Him. The Christian life is a step-by-step pursuit to know Jesus better. Dietrich Bonhoeffer said, "Christianity without discipleship is always Christianity without Christ." If we have no desire to follow Him and no desire to know Him more intimately, then we really have no basis to claim Christianity.

Everyone who has heard and answered the call to follow Jesus knows that the work of the Holy Spirit doesn't end with introducing us to Jesus; the Holy Spirit also creates a longing in us to know Jesus. That identifies His work in our lives. He intensifies our hunger for Jesus, He reveals His footsteps to us, then He empowers us to follow. That is the daily life of a disciple. 1 John 2:6 says, "The one who says he abides in Him ought himself to walk in the same manner as He walked." I want to experience the closeness that is abiding in Him, and as a result of that continuing closeness, I want to walk as He walked.

Paul the Apostle summed up the primary longing of his life in one simple phrase: "That I may know Him" (Phil. 3:10 KJV). With five basic words, Paul exposed the existence of a hidden need in his life—an unsatisfied longing. If he had never said it out loud, no one would have ever known. No one would have ever associated Paul with a need to know Jesus. Had we observed his life, we would have concluded that he couldn't possibly be closer to Jesus. Had we spent time with him, listening to his conversations, hearing his prayers, and witnessing his sacrificial life, we would have said, "that man really knows Jesus." You can't say the things he says and do the things he does and suffer all that he suffers unless you really know Him. However, Paul didn't hesitate to publicly confess, "I want to know Jesus more." He wanted to know Him not only in the power of His resurrection, but also in the fellowship of His suffering.

Paul was confessing his willingness to do anything or to go through anything if it meant knowing Jesus more.

That was how badly Paul wanted to know Jesus. Nothing else would satisfy that longing in him. He wasn't focused on the fact that he was approaching the end of his life. He wasn't focused on all the churches he had successfully planted, or how effectively he had advanced the gospel into territories that were once hostile to the gospel. He wasn't even focused on how much of the New Testament he had been privileged to write. After all that he had accomplished and experienced, his focus was still on having a deeper, more meaningful experiential knowledge of Jesus.

Paul wanted more than anything else to know Jesus more. That should sound absolutely crazy to us because we know that Paul met Jesus on the road to Damascus (Acts 9:3–7). We know that he even heard Jesus' voice and spoke with Him. Paul experienced all that, but what we also understand is that his miraculous salvation experience wasn't enough. This man who was privileged to be in Jesus' presence wasn't satisfied by merely being in His presence. It wasn't that he didn't know Jesus at all. Of course he knew Him. He knew Jesus' gospel because it radically transformed his life. Paul knew Jesus' protection because He guarded him on his missionary journeys. He knew Jesus' sufficient grace because it strengthened him when he battled his thorn in the flesh. He knew Jesus' power because it had empowered him to perform supernatural miracles. So, his confession wasn't about knowing Jesus—it was about wanting to know Jesus more.

For Paul, everything in his life outside of knowing Jesus more was secondary. He said that himself: "Indeed, I count everything as loss because of the surpassing worth of knowing Christ Jesus my Lord. For his sake I have suffered the loss of all things and count them as rubbish, in order that I may gain Christ" (Phil. 3:8). To Paul, nothing else really mattered. Knowing Jesus was more valuable than anything else in his life. That was his greatest aspiration—knowing Jesus. His desire for that intimate relationship was so transcendent that he was willing to discard everything else. Nothing else mattered when it was compared to really, intimately knowing Jesus more.

Paul's desire wasn't to make Jesus' acquaintance or enjoy a casual friendship. He didn't even express a desire to know more and more about Jesus. His intention was clear. He wasn't on a quest to know "about" Jesus; he wanted to know Jesus. *The Pulpit Commentary* says, "the knowledge here spoken of is a personal knowledge, gained, not by hearing or reading, but by direct personal communion with the Lord." That's what Paul was longing for when he said, "that I may know Him." He wanted a more intimate, more experiential relationship with Jesus. He wanted a deeper level of communion with Jesus. He wanted increased personal contact with Jesus.

Paul knew a deeper relationship with Jesus was necessary for him if he was going to impersonate Jesus accurately. He knew that was the only way the people he rubbed shoulders with, and shared jail cells with, were ever going to see Jesus. Paul wanted to know Jesus intimately so he could be like Jesus practically. That's why he had to know Him. Seven verses after confessing his desire to know Jesus more, Paul said to the church, "join in imitating me." This was an invitation for them to impersonate him in desiring to be like Jesus. Paul wanted others to live with an overwhelming desire to know Jesus so that in knowing Jesus, they could live to make Jesus known.

J. Sidlow Baxter wrote, "Christ Himself is the supreme object of the believer's desire, the true goal of our whole life and being. How true it is that those who give up most for Christ, love Him most dearly and possess Him most satisfyingly!" What a convicting challenge! None of us should be able to read those words without feeling the need to question our own affections. Is Jesus truly the supreme object of our desire? Is He our one true goal? What are we willing to give up in order to have more of Him? How much are we willing to give up if it means knowing Him more? These are the kind of heart-searching questions Paul's confession leads me to wrestle with.

I want to be able to honestly say, "Jesus, I want to know you more," but at the same time, I realize my desire for a more intimate relationship with Him needs to increase drastically. I don't want to be satisfied to merely possess information about Jesus. I don't want to be satisfied just to know who He is. I don't want to be content with brief moments of religious activity in His name. I want to be a follower of Jesus who is never satisfied with the distance between Him and me. I want to be and I want you to be, people who long to know Him more intimately so we can make Him known more clearly. May Jesus be our highest priority, and may we realize that anything less will never make Him visible through our lives. Watchman Née wrote in his book, *The Normal Christian Life*, "The idea of waste only comes into our Christianity when we underestimate the worth of our Lord."

Knowing Jesus requires sacrifice, but knowing Him is life's greatest satisfaction. If we really long to make Him visible, we have to pursue Him, with a passion to know Him. We can't waste our Christianity pursuing things with little or no value, but rather, we have to live in pursuit of heaven's greatest treasure, Jesus. He will never be visible to them until He is visible to us, and He will never be visible to us until we pursue Him with all our hearts. Jesus has to be our greatest desire. Knowing Him and making Him known must be our one, true goal. We will never effectively impersonate Him until we experientially know Him, and we will never experientially know Him until we determine to live our lives covered by the dust from His feet.

PRAYER

God help us to make Jesus our greatest affection. Create in us a hunger for Him. A persistent hunger to know Him more and a refusal to be satisfied by anything else. May Jesus be our greatest priority, and knowing Jesus intimately our greatest pursuit. Make His footprints clear to us and following in His footprints preeminent to us. May we get to the place where we're so close to Him that our lives start to resemble His life. Equip us to be great impersonators of Jesus so that everyone who encounters us will know that they have encountered Him. In Jesus' name, Amen!

REFLECT

1. How familiar are you with the characteristics of Jesus? Which ones do you see the Holy Spirit developing in your life, and which ones are lacking?

2. Are you following Jesus closely enough to be covered in the dust from His feet? What do you allow to take priority over spending time with Him?

3. What unseen sin do you most closely guard in your life? How does that sin repeatedly create distance between you and Jesus?

4. What are you doing currently to experience increased closeness with Jesus?

5. For Paul, "that I may know Him" defined the primary pursuit of His life. If you honestly filled in the blank, what would be the primary pursuit of your life? That I may _____

"*Bad evangelism says: I'm right, you're wrong, and I would love to tell you about it.*"

Timothy Keller

CHAPTER 3

TALK TO WHOMEVER, WHEREVER, WHENEVER

I magine all the different things God could have used to reveal Jesus to the world. He could have easily made the blue skies His scroll and written the story of Jesus in the clouds, or given the oceans a voice so that with every crashing wave, the message of Jesus was told over and over again. God could have created the birds with the ability to sing beautiful songs about Jesus from every tree branch and every rooftop, but He didn't. God didn't choose the stars or the planets, the animals or the plants, but He chose to make Jesus visible through us. He decided to use flawed human beings to make His perfect Son known. We are the only thing in all creation that has been given the gift of speech. Nothing else on our planet has the ability to talk about His greatness or broadcast the news of His goodness. According to Ephesians 2:10, "We are His workmanship, created in Christ Jesus for good works." We are the ones who have been created to increase the volume of the gospel throughout the world. We are responsible for that good work.

Every sinner who has been redeemed by the grace of God, and declared righteous by God, has also been empowered and employed by God to make His Son known throughout the world. That is the assignment that has been given to everyone who has been created in Christ Jesus, and living into that assignment requires using the physical strengths and unique abilities that God has given exclusively to the human race. The greatest of these abilities is our ability to communicate. Nothing else in all God's creation was given that gift. Each time we open our mouths and speak a word, we are enjoying a gift given to us by God. Each time we hear someone speak, and their speech allows us to know what they want, who they are, what they are thinking, or what they want us to know, we are enjoying a gift given to us by God.

Virtually everything in our world revolves around communication. Books, signs, television, radio, cell phones, computers, and music all have one thing in common: they are all an expression of our desire to communicate. So why was this amazing gift only given to humans? Why are we the only thing on the earth that expresses our thoughts, dreams, hurts, desires, and experiences with words? It's because we are the only thing in all creation made in God's image. Genesis 1:3 begins with the words "and God said." No sooner than we are introduced to God in the Bible, we hear Him speaking. God speaks into lifelessness and calls forth life, but it wasn't until He formed man that something spoke back. Speech was exclusive to God; God made speech exclusive to us because we were the only thing created in His image. We are also the only thing He died to save. John 3:16 says, "for God so loved the world that He gave His only begotten Son that whosoever believes in Him should not perish but have everlasting life." The gift of Jesus was given for whosoever, not whatsoever. That means we are the only ones in all creation that can communicate the message of the gospel to the only ones Jesus died to save, but that will only happen if we use our gift from God, for God. We must see that our ability to communicate is the most powerful tool we have to advance the message of the gospel. Visible Jesus requires us to open our mouths and make Jesus known. It means refusing to let our faith in Jesus remain invisible in our conversations.

Too many Christians are like camouflage. They blend into their surroundings. They adapt to the environment around them. You can look in their vicinity and still not see them. Rather than impacting their surroundings by making Jesus visible, they intentionally look like everyone else, and sadly, that is true, regardless of how dark the environment might be. "Christians" in our culture seem to live down to their surroundings. The deeper and darker the world becomes, the deeper and darker they become. Paul asked the questions in 2 Corinthians 6:14, "What does a believer have in common with an unbeliever? What fellowship does light have with darkness?" He was asking, how a can believer look, act, talk, behave, and live like an unbeliever with no noticeable difference between the two? How can a believer associate with an unbeliever and appear to be exactly the same?

Three verses later Paul followed those questions with a charge, "come out from among them and be separate." He was calling on the Christians in Corinth to make sure they were distinguishable from the rest of the world. They were to be unlike the sinful culture around them. They were supposed to look and sound differently. Their conduct—as well as their conversations—was to be different. Following Jesus required them to live outside of the shadows. It required them to take off their cultural camouflage and be noticeably different. Their lives were to be more like a blaze orange vest and less like a pair of camouflaged coveralls, and just as that was God's expectation for them, that is God's expectation for us.

The way we communicate through our lives and our words should make us identifiable. Peter stood by the fireside, and even when He was trying to curse, His speech betrayed Him. He couldn't help but sound like a follower of Jesus. He was making the biggest mistake of his life, and even then, people were saying, "You're one of Jesus' followers." He couldn't help it. He stood out. We should stand out. Our speech should betray us. Titus 2:14 makes it clear that we are supposed to live differently, and every day we live blending in with the world around us is a day wasted, because it's another day of failing to make Jesus visible.

Living differently is never easy because it makes us more obvious. Most people naturally prefer obscurity. Life is easier for those who learn to be like cultural chameleons. They are able to blend in with their surroundings and remain undetected and unnoticed. There is a certain sense of safety in living like that. Very few people are offended by tolerance and conformity. That is why most people spend the majority of their lives trying to fit in. Most of us don't like being called average, but at the same time, average becomes our security blanket.

Average allows us to disappear, and as long as we dress the same, talk the same, and live and act the same, no one will ever single us out. Occasionally, we do see that one person who embraces being odd. That person who doesn't care what the current trends are or doesn't mind strange looks. That person who doesn't live under the control of public opinion. But when we see that person who dares to be different, our reaction is always the same—we stare. The reason we stare is that he or she is not like everyone else, and we all know that's the response you can expect when you are different.

The only time we have any interest in being obvious is when we have the opportunity to highlight an accomplishment, talent, ability, or appealing feature. That is so much easier for us than highlighting our belief in the Bible or making it known that we have placed our faith in the person and work of Jesus Christ. Because the moment we identify ourselves with Jesus, we are marked. We no longer have the comfort of anonymity and neutrality. Being known as the great employee who gets along with everyone is easier than being known as the employee who believes in and lives for Jesus. Being known as popular or cool at your local high school is so much easier than being known as a fully devoted follower of Christ. Life is easier when we remain silent about our countercultural beliefs. Life is easier when we have a loose association with religion or we choose to make our faith a private matter. The exact opposite is true when we live to make Jesus visible. It requires us to walk differently, and it requires us to talk differently.

Instead of going along with the crowd, we live against the grain, and that is never easy. Fitting in with the world around us can no longer be our goal. Being the kind of Christian described in 2 Peter 1:5–8 becomes our goal, and being that kind of Christian means being different. Because when we take on the characteristics described in 2 Peter 1:5–8, we will stand in stark contrast with the rest of the world. The end result of being shaped by the word of God instead of the culture is being less like the culture and more like Jesus. When we start exemplifying godly attributes like faith, virtue, a strong knowledge of God's word, self-control, steadfastness, godliness, and love, we will stand out from the crowd. These attributes, like the fruit of the Spirit, are only produced by the Spirit in the life of a believer. By default, the work of the Spirit in our lives makes us look, live, and talk differently. If that work is not happening in our lives, then the Spirit is not in us.

Maybe you're asking, "What if I don't want to be different?" or "What if I would rather be an obscure Christian?" The Apostle Peter answered those kinds of questions with a firm answer. He said, "You are nearsighted, blind and forgetful of the fact that Jesus has cleansed you from your former sins." Which means that failing to live to make Jesus visible is failing to live for the very reason Jesus saved us. Salvation has never been about securing a ticket to heaven. That is certainly a benefit, but that is not the reason. If that were the reason, the moment we were saved, God would transport us to heaven and add our voices to the millions of others crying, "holy, holy, holy." He doesn't immediately take us out of the world because He has a greater purpose. God saves us and leaves us in a hostile, Christ-less environment so that we can make Jesus visible to people who aren't saved. If we weren't in the world, the world would never see Jesus. So everywhere I am, and to everyone I'm with, I have the unique ability to make Jesus visible. Believing that ultimately changes the way we view our geographical location and our role in impacting it. We stop believing we are where we are by accident, and we start believing that we are where we are for a purpose. That purpose is always to show and share Jesus through our words and actions. Our location never changes our mission, which is to make Jesus visible wherever we are and to whomever we are with.

The Earth's surface is approximately 197 million square miles, and is home to 7.4 billion people. Quoting those numbers doesn't mean that I fully understand their implications, but I do understand that the Earth is an enormous and incredibly crowded place. That's why it amazes me to think that the sovereign God of the universe is so intimately aware of me that He can put me in front of just the right person at just the right time in just the right place. He doesn't unrealistically expect me to make Jesus visible everywhere. That would be impossible! He just expects me to make Jesus visible in my immediate geography—the space around me. He needs me and you to be like the old Coleman lanterns that my daddy used to use.

We don't have to be capable of lighting up the entire riverbank, or the whole campsite, we just need to light up the riverbank or the campsite around us. Our focus should be on the people around us, not on the people we may never encounter. Missions can't be just giving money in an offering to reach the people "out there"; missions must be living to impact the people "right here." The people who long to make Jesus visible get that. They see themselves as missionaries and the people around them as their mission field. It doesn't matter where they are; their agenda remains unchanged. The people who long to make Jesus visible frequently ask these questions: Why does God have me right here, right now? Why does God have me around these people? Why has God allowed me to be in this situation? The answer is because Proverbs 3:6 is true. He will direct your path.

I personally experienced that just outside of Sturgis, South Dakota. My wife, our oldest daughter, and I were on our way back from a road trip to Yellowstone National Park. The trip had been everything we had hoped it would be. The views in every state had been spectacular, the weather had been perfect, and the opportunity to chauffeur our daughter on her senior trip had been a priceless treasure. The trip had seemed almost too good to be true. We had been there, we had done that, and we were ready to get back home to see our other daughters. Unfortunately, our van wasn't going to cooperate with our plan. We had just driven over the massive Big Horn Mountain and made our way into the barren Black Hills National Forest when our van started severely overheating. I would stop, let it cool down, add water to the radiator and drive only a few hundred feet before it would overheat again.

Finally, and I mean finally around 11:00 p.m., we made it to a McDonald's. Thank God we did, because the moment we pulled into a parking space, our water pump exploded. After a few minutes on the phone with a friend, I was able to get a hold of a gracious pastor who lived nearby. He believed in Galatians 6:10 and kindly offered to help. In no time at all, he reached the McDonald's where we were stranded and guided us to a nearby garage. Had it been any further, we wouldn't have been able to make it. Our van was making clanking noises that we had never heard before. The temperature gauge was buried in the red, smoke was billowing out from under the hood, and just when we thought we couldn't make it any further, we reached the garage parking lot safe and sound.

So there we were, broken down in Rapid City, South Dakota, during Sturgis' seventy-fifth anniversary celebration. Over one million rowdy bikers from all over the country packed into that one area to celebrate their love for motorcycles. There were no hotel rooms available anywhere, and even if there had been, the rates were quadrupled. That was our predicament. We had been in our van all day long, and at that moment we were accepting the fact that we were going to have to be in our van all night as well. That was not one of our better moments. We were frustrated, tired, concerned, and discouraged. We did our best to recline the seats and rest, but with the sounds of loud motorcycles and screaming sirens, it was a long, miserable night.

The next morning, the moment the garage opened, we walked inside with our wrinkled clothes, messed up hair, puffy eyes, and full bladders, and started pleading for help. The owner of the garage assured us he would get to our vehicle as quickly as possible, but in the meantime, we were welcomed to wait in the seating area. Needless to say, this wasn't our brightest spiritual moment, and we weren't at our best. We were aggravated with the situation, worried about the cost, frustrated with each other, and ready to get home. Not for a second were we asking, God, why are we here and why is this happening? We just wanted to live the words of Willie Nelson and get on the road again. At that point, we didn't know that we were moments away from meeting Cindy.

Cindy was the woman the auto parts store had sent to deliver the water pump we needed for our van. She was around fifty years old, with sandy blonde hair, and she was wearing a faded uniform shirt with cut-off sleeves along with a pair of jeans. She had a bold laugh that filled the garage's waiting room and an even bolder compassion that touched our hearts. Although she had never met us, the moment the garage owner told her about our trouble, she came over to where we were sitting and offered to cook dinner for us that night if we were still in town. We were in awe of her generous offer to invite us into her home. I made sure to let her know how much we appreciated her willingness to be kind to us, but let her know we would be leaving town as soon as our van was repaired. She assured us that if we were forced to change our plans, her offer would still be good. I thanked her once again for her kindness, and in passing, I mentioned the strength we find in God's grace. I expressed my appreciation for God's goodness and my awareness that our problem was small when compared to the problems of others. That one comment opened the door for Cindy to tearfully share the trial her own family was facing.

Over the next few minutes, Cindy shared with us the painful crisis that she was currently going through. She had offered to help us, but in all honesty, she needed help herself. So there in the middle of the garage waiting area, Cindy told us her story. She explained to us that she was delivering auto parts because she needed the money to take care of her grandchildren. The reason she had to take care of them was due to the fact that her twenty-eight-year-old son-in-law was battling terminal cancer, and in trying to care for him, Cindy's daughter had lost her job. So, there they were, three children, a terminal cancer diagnosis, and no financial income. Cindy was working hard and doing her best, but the burden was heavy. For the past several months, she had had the children full-time because her daughter and her son-in-law had been hours away at a cancer treatment facility. With little money, and no help, Cindy was trying to hold it all together. That's what she was living through at that exact moment, and because of God's divine providence, she was standing right in front of me. That's when God elbowed me and reminded me that being tired, dirty, and in a bad mood didn't relieve me of my responsibility to make Jesus visible.

When Cindy had finished sharing her story, I started sharing with her the good news that Jesus cares for us even in our crisis situations. I reminded Cindy that Jesus had suffered for us on the cross and that He was capable of identifying with our deepest pain. I was able to say that Jesus is always enough. Yes, our trials can be overwhelming, but even then, Jesus is enough. Tears flowed down Cindy's face when she heard those words. It was obvious that through our conversation about Jesus' suffering and His limitless grace that God had encouraged her heart. We had only known her for a few minutes, but the hugs we exchanged following our conversation made us feel as if we had known her for a lifetime. The next Sunday, I shared Cindy's story with our Hope Church family, and after hearing all that she was going through, they gave about $3,000 to help her care for her family. Cindy's story reminds me that God is always at work, and as a Christian, I should be too.

God had me exactly where He wanted me. He determined the route that I would take leaving Yellowstone. God made sure our van started having trouble before we left the park so we would choose to go in a different direction. He knew each time our van overheated and our trip was prolonged. He knew every moment before and during our trip. God was the One who allowed us to make it to Rapid City, South Dakota, and He was the One who made sure we were right around the corner from the garage where Cindy would be making deliveries. He even made sure that no auto parts store in the area had the water pump we needed except for the one where Cindy worked. God did all that! It is easy to see when looking back that it was God who sovereignly orchestrated every mile and moment. It was God who knew that we needed to meet Cindy and that Cindy needed to see Jesus. God had intentionally placed my family there to make Jesus visible to a struggling woman who desperately needed to see Him.

I had another one of those encounters one night in Myrtle Beach, South Carolina, on a family vacation. After taking a little late-night walk along the beach, we finally got back to our room and started settling in for some TV and relaxation. That's when my daughter decided to say, "Oh yeah, when we were walking down the beach tonight, one of my sandals came off." We exclaimed, What? You didn't say anything? You didn't pick it up? Denise quickly chimed in and said, "but those sandals were brand new!" I knew what was coming next and I was right. She said, "Brian will you go down to the beach and see if you can find her sandal?" I was not happy! Are you kidding me? Which one of my superhero powers do you suggest I use to find a brown sandal on a brown sandy beach at 11:30 p.m.? I was furious! It was all ridiculous. It was ridiculous that she didn't say something the moment it slipped off, it was ridiculous that she waited until we had walked all the way back to our hotel room and gotten settled. It was ridiculous that they actually thought I could find it, and it was ridiculous that my wife's "persistent encouragement" convinced me to go and look.

I mumbled all the way to the elevator, all the way out to the beach, and all the way down the beach. My daughter heard every word because I made her walk with me to look for the sandal since she was the one who lost it. I'm sure she would have rather been anywhere other than there because I was giving her an earful every step of the way. Finally, we reached a small white fence line, and she said, "Daddy, this looks like the place." So, our walking ended, and our searching was officially underway. Our mission was to find one small sandal on the South Carolina coastline. Our only lead was the word of the little girl who lost it, and she was standing there confused about whether or not we were in the right place.

In that moment of frustration, we were so busy looking for the lost sandal, that we didn't even notice a group of young adults surf fishing right beside of us. However, one of them did notice us. He walked over to where we were and asked, "Did you lose something—do you need some help?" My response was, "We need all the help we can get." I reached out to shake the hand of the heavily tattooed young man and said, "My name is Brian." He introduced himself as Hank, and after a couple of minutes of small talk, we both started carefully searching through the sand as if we were hunting for a lost treasure. I admit that I was so focused on finding the lost sandal that I was a little slow getting God's message, but during our search, God spoke to my heart and said, "Hank is why you're here. You need to talk to him, about me."

The God of the universe reminded me on the beach that night that He could have had me anywhere. There are 197 million square miles, after all. He reminded me that He could have had me talking to anybody. There are 7.4 billion people, after all. He reminded me that where I was, and who I was with, wasn't a matter of chance. God had me where Hank was, at the same time Hank was there by design. It wasn't by accident that Hank was the only one who left the crowd of young adults to help us search for the missing sandal. That night was a divine appointment on the calendar of God. "Hey Hank, what do you believe about Jesus?" was the question I asked. The searching immediately stopped! It felt like everything around us went silent. Hank looked up as if he was glad I had asked.

The conversation about his spiritual condition was easy. He was an open book. He shared how far in the wrong direction his life had gone. He told me about his battle with addiction, and the other demons in his life. He shared his history of growing up in a dysfunctional, broken family. He said he knew more than anything that he needed to make things right with God. He said he knew his problems were beyond him. We talked for a long time that night on the beach, and I used every word and every sentence to point Hank to Jesus. God was definitely at work that night. He had to be. Hank wasn't in a hurry to get back to fishing. He wasn't even distracted by all the guys and girls he was fishing with. Hank listened intently, and was clearly moved that night as I said, "You will never get things straightened out on your own; Jesus is your only hope."

Eventually, we found the sandal, but the sandal didn't matter anymore. Honestly, I was glad that it had been lost because it was that lost sandal that led to a lost soul having an unlikely, unexpected encounter with the gospel. I walked away that night amazed that the God who controls everything had been walking down the beach with us. He was the one who allowed a sandal to slip off of a little girl's foot at just the right place, and He knew exactly where it needed to be lost. He even allowed my daughter to be silent about losing her sandal just long enough for Hank to reach the exact spot where our search would take place. God had been in control of every detail. God had orchestrated our times and locations so Hank could see Jesus that night on the beach. He wasn't even thinking about God, but God was thinking about him. I wasn't thinking about making Jesus visible, but I was the one that God trusted with that moment.

Once I fully realized all that God had done to make that moment happen, I couldn't stop talking about it. The same little girl who had heard me fuss all the way down the beach, heard me say over and over again on our way back up the beach, "God is awesome!" "God did this!" "God needed your sandal to be lost so Daddy could talk to Hank about Jesus!" It was true; God had created that moment. God is constantly creating moments.

Those kinds of opportunities happen every day. God places "Cindys" and "Hanks" in all our paths. God allows us to encounter people every day who are far away from Him. The problem is, we typically overlook those moments. Far too often we are self-absorbed, occupied, and distracted. If we could only see the storyboard of our lives, maybe then we would realize how frequently it's dominated by missed opportunities, because all us have had missed opportunities. All us have had times when we should have said something, or when we should have served, or when we should have reached out, or when we should have offered to pray. I know that because it happened to me one night in a Manhattan hotel. Denise and I had just reached our room after a long day of traveling; it was late, and I was ready for bed. I had just laid down when I heard her ask, "Brian, would you please go to the ice machine for me?" To be honest, I really didn't want to go, but I got up, got dressed, and headed down the hallway. I don't believe it was by accident that another man reached the ice machine at the same exact time that I did. I invited him to get his ice first and asked him how he was doing. He looked down at the floor and softly answered, "honestly, not that well." That was a wide-open door. All I had to do was walk through it. I should have looked back at him and said, "There is someone who loves us even on the days we're not doing well." I should have asked, "Do you mind if I pray for you?" I should have said something about Jesus. I should have shown him that the hope of the world was alive in me, but instead, I opened my mouth and said, "I hope tomorrow will be better." A broken man was standing in front of me, and that was all I said. I had only taken a few steps toward my room when God broke my heart.

At that moment, I felt the full weight of my failure. What had I done? Why didn't I at least mention Jesus? I turned and quickly headed back to the ice machine whispering the prayer, "please still be there, please still be there," but when I reached the ice machine, the man was nowhere to be found. God had given me a visible Jesus opportunity, and I hadn't made Jesus visible. I walked back to my room in tears. I prayed and begged God to forgive me, but it didn't give me back that moment. I had lived Earnest Worker's convicting statement, "The halfway Christian is a torment to himself and of no benefit to others." That's why I'm saying to you; don't miss the moments that God gives you every single day. Don't fail to make Jesus visible.

The people you work with, the people at the campsite next to yours, the person sitting next to you in the doctor's office, the waitress at your local diner, the mechanic who works on your car, the elderly couple in your neighborhood who feels alone, the people who frequent the local Salvation Army, or even your own family all have one thing in common: they need to see Jesus. Don't fail to show them Jesus! You will either carry with you the satisfaction of knowing that you displayed Jesus in front of them or the regret of knowing that you were of no spiritual value to the people that God placed in your path. You aren't with those around you by accident. God intentionally schedules appointments for you and me to make Jesus visible to the people around us, but we have to open our mouths and talk.

In Acts 8:26–39 it was God who took Philip away from the crowds in the villages of Samaria near Jerusalem. It was God who placed him near the chariot that an

Ethiopian eunuch was riding in. It was God who knew the eunuch was looking through the writings of the prophet Isaiah, unable to understand what he was reading. It was God who had been preparing the eunuch's heart to receive the gospel. It was God who supernaturally placed Philip at the eunuch's exact location while he was reading exactly the right verses. It was God who gave Philip the opportunity to make Jesus visible.

God didn't need Philip to do what only He could do. God just needed Philip to take the words of the prophet Isaiah and point the Ethiopian eunuch to Jesus. Thank God Philip didn't try to impress the eunuch with a history lesson on Isaiah's life and times, or overwhelm him with a complete overview of Isaiah's prophecy. Philip merely served as a road sign and pointed the eunuch to Jesus. A few moments later the eunuch said, "Here is water! What prevents me from being baptized?" He was asking, "is there anything else I need to do to be baptized? I want this to be official." Philip said, "if you believe with all your heart, you can." The eunuch responded with the bold confession, "I believe that Jesus Christ is the Son of God." Obviously, that was all that needed to be said. The chariot stopped at the eunuch's command, he and Philip waded into the water, and he was baptized.

What an amazing moment! God had placed two people in the same location at exactly the right time and determined this beautiful outcome—but why? Why had God taken Philip away from a place where mass amounts of people were being saved in order to send him to one person? From a numerical perspective, it looks as if God thought too small, but from God's perspective, He looked beyond the one and saw the gospel reaching an unreached nation.

Ethiopia at that time was still without the gospel. God knew by saving the eunuch, the gospel would be advanced beyond its current borders. The eunuch would make Jesus visible to people who otherwise wouldn't know what He looked like. God was painting a bigger picture. John Dick wrote in his commentary, Lectures on the Acts of the Apostles,

> It does not appear, that in Jerusalem the Ethiopian eunuch had heard anything about Christ. He had now left that city and had advanced so far in his journey that he was entering into countries where the good news of salvation had not been published. He was passing the boundary which separated light from darkness and returning, without the knowledge of the Savior, to his own land, where he could not have obtained it by ordinary means. At this critical moment, a minister of Jesus was sent, by the special direction of the Spirit, to speak words by which his soul should be saved.

That was God's purpose. From His vantage point, He was able to see beyond the crowds that were gathered in Samaria and Jerusalem. He was able to see those who would be saved in Ethiopia. He was able to see those who would be reached in every city the eunuch visited. Acts 8 is the story of God making a divine appointment on the calendar of time, for the purpose of increasing the volume and the visibility of the gospel. Acts 8 is a reminder that addition can quickly lead to multiplication. When one person makes Jesus visible to another, who then makes Jesus visible to another, there is no way to measure the future results. One moment, one person, one encounter can have enormous, eternal impact.

G. Campbell Morgan wrote in his book, *The Acts of The Apostles,*

> He was at work by the Spirit in the heart of the Ethiopian eunuch before Philip reached him. The Spirit was ahead of Philip, making this man discontented, giving him to know his own ignorance. So, we see Christ preparing this Ethiopian eunuch; commanding His servant to leave the city for the desert, the crowds for loneliness, the fellowship for isolation. As we see the meeting between these two men, we realize anew that this Christ is He Who opens, and no man shuts; Who shuts, and no man opens. He is still carrying on these same things in these same ways. He opens doors, and then through His people, enters the doors He opens.

One man named Philip made Jesus visible to one Ethiopian eunuch, and the outcome was the gospel being carried to a nation. The eunuch had access to the palace and the villages. He had influence with royalty and with servants. He would have had the opportunity to share the story of his conversion with the rich and the poor. Jesus was made visible to him, and he would be able to make Jesus visible to others. People that Philip would never encounter would see Jesus because Philip was obedient to make Jesus visible. That's how God works! He reaches people by reaching people. His plan has always been to save more people by saving more people. Every person who is changed by the gospel is called to advance the gospel beyond themselves. That is God's plan to reach the world.

The exciting news is, Acts 8 doesn't have to be exclusive to Philip. You and I can have Acts 8 experiences. The spirit of Christ that empowered Philip is the same spirit of Christ that resides inside of us. Philippians 2:13 is still true when it says, "it is God who works in you [us], both to will and to work for His good pleasure." God still works through us to accomplish His eternal purpose. He hasn't lost any of His power or appeal. He hasn't weakened in His ability to save. He hasn't forfeited His capability to multiply a moment. What happens in the moment is never confined to the moment when we live to make Jesus visible. God can take our visible Jesus moments and use them to impact the masses.

Dr. Mordecai Ham didn't know when he was preaching at a Charlotte, North Carolina, crusade that a young man named Billy Graham was sitting behind him in the choir. Billy wasn't in the choir because he loved to sing; he admitted that he couldn't sing at all. Billy was only back there because he was convinced that Dr. Ham had been preaching directly to him. After a restless night of deep conviction, he had convinced himself that if he sat behind Dr. Ham in the choir, those feelings of conviction wouldn't be as strong. In the end, Billy Graham couldn't escape God's persistent call to salvation, not even in the choir loft. That night, he left his inconspicuous seat in the choir to kneel down in the sawdust to call out to Jesus for salvation. He didn't walk to the prayer altar that night longing to see Mordecai Ham; he longed to see Jesus. The Holy Spirit had made the gospel believable to Billy Graham, and only Jesus could satisfy the longing of his soul. He says that night his hero changed from Babe Ruth to Jesus. That is because it was Jesus who changed Billy Graham's life.

Mordecai Ham had only been faithful to make Jesus visible. He didn't know the young man kneeling at the altar that night would eventually preach the gospel to the world, but God knew. He didn't know that the young man who was receiving Jesus within his reach would make Jesus visible to millions of people far beyond his reach, but God knew—and God still knows. God knows who will encounter Jesus through you. He knows who will experience salvation after hearing you share the gospel. He knows who will fall in love with Jesus because you put Him on display. He knows! And He also knows who will experience salvation as a result of the person who encountered Jesus through you. God knows the reach of your visible Jesus moments. He knows who will be impacted when you light up the dark spaces around you.

When you look across your backyard on a summer's night, you don't see the thousands of bugs that are flying all around you. They all navigate the night sky virtually undetected. The only bugs you really notice are the lightning bugs. That is because each one of them is equipped with a bulb, and bioluminescence gives them the unique ability to make a dark field look as if it is decorated for Christmas. I have always found it impossible not to watch them. The backdrop of the night sky makes their flickers of light so conspicuous. You can't help but notice each time they illuminate a tiny fragment of the immense darkness that surrounds them. In reality, they produce very little light. Virtually every other light source has the power to render their light invisible, which means we don't notice lightning bugs because of the power of their light, but rather because of the depth of the darkness. It isn't their brightness that demands our attention; it's the darkness that makes their tiny light impossible to ignore. I'm sharing this example because I think all of us look at the overwhelming darkness of the world we're living in, and we think, what can I do?

There is no doubt we are living in extremely dark times. We are morally shipwrecked, spiritually apathetic, relationally broken, governmentally corrupt, and socially divided—these are extraordinarily dark times, and instead of being inspired by the darkness, we're being discouraged. We're not looking into the darkness and realizing the need for light, we're looking into the darkness and questioning, "What's the use?" We should know that even the smallest glimmer of light is noticeable when everything is dark. That should be encouraging to us because it means that every single one of us has an opportunity to make our light count. We need to stop constantly complaining about the darkness and pointing out the darkness, and we need to start using our lives and our voices to impact the darkness. We might just be one tiny light in a world of immense darkness, but if we use our conversations to speak light, and our lives to shine light, we can be sure that our light will be seen.

Our lives should resemble the lives of those who were first called Christians. They were truly successful disciples. They resembled Jesus so much that they were accused of resembling Jesus. That is so foreign in our culture. The idea that the people in Antioch could look at these believers and see Jesus in their lives is hard for us to understand. Remember our culture promotes having shared style, shared ideals, shared beliefs, shared tolerances, and shared values. The Bible promotes living to the glory of God, in obedience to God regardless of what the culture is doing or promoting. Had the believers in Antioch looked and lived like the culture in Antioch, no one would have identified them any differently.

Before Acts 11:26, no one had ever been referred to as a Christian. Followers of Jesus were typically referred to as "those of the way," or some people would scorn or attempt to insult them by calling them "Nazarenes." Those inside of the Christian community called one another "believers" or "brethren." So what was it about the lives of those believers in Antioch that caused someone to say for the first time, "these people are like Jesus Christ?"

Their attributes and actions are clearly recorded in this chapter, but they seem so ordinary that we fail to notice. Acts 11:20 says they were "preaching the Lord Jesus," which means they were openly communicating the message of the gospel of Jesus with the non-believers in Antioch. Acts 11:21 says, "the hand of the Lord was with them, and a great number who believed turned to the Lord." They were faithfully sharing the gospel, and God was faithfully using the gospel to change people's lives. Acts 11:23 lets us know that not only were they preaching, but they were also living out the grace of God, and being faithful to the purpose of God.

Acts 11:26 offers us one final bit of information by letting us know that they were also meeting together and learning together as the Church. Nothing they were doing was miraculous or impossible. They weren't called Christians because they were performing the supernatural; they were called Christians because they were exemplifying Christian life. They weren't doing anything that we aren't capable of doing. If we would share Jesus with the people around us, if we would seek to have God's hand on our lives, if we would live for the purpose of God and faithfully meet together with the people of God, more people would identify us as Christians. What the people in Antioch saw and heard made them say of those believers, "they are like Jesus," but it started with those believers being willing to open their mouths and talk about Jesus.

That is what must happen. We have to start including Jesus in our conversations, we have to start revealing Jesus through our lives, and we have to start being willing to serve our neighbors in His name. We have to be obedient to live by His commandments, and actively show the outrageous love of Jesus to people who are not like us. We have to unceasingly strive to live holy and blameless lives. That's what it means to live differently. It means taking God's word off of pages and putting it on the pavement, and that is the only way we will ever make a difference. We embrace the "Cindys" that God places in our paths, and we talk to them about Jesus. We engage the "Hanks" that God puts in front of us, and we talk to them about Jesus. We serve the poor, and we talk to them about Jesus. That is the only way we can shine our light into the darkness. We live differently, and we talk differently because we are different.

Virtually every child who grew up in Sunday school learned, "this little light of mine, I'm gonna let it shine." That song was written from an incredible truth shared by Jesus in Matthew 5:14–15. Jesus said to His followers, "you are the light of the world. A city that is set on a hill cannot be hidden." I read this, and I immediately think of driving into New York City at night. There are lights everywhere. As a matter of fact, you see the lights of the city long before you reach the city. There are so many lights they actually cause the sky above the city to appear as if it's glowing. I read this verse, and I imagine New York City on a hill with every light in the city shining. No one could possibly miss it. No one would be able to ignore it. Jesus said to His followers, I want that to be you—I want you to be like a city on a hill with every torch lit, with a candle burning in every window—I want you to be eye-catching, I want you to be unmissable. He then went on to say, "nor do people light a lamp and put it under a basket, but on a stand." Jesus was giving His followers these examples to communicate the importance of being obvious. He was letting them know His desire for them was to be everything but invisible. Jesus was saying to them and us, I want you to shine, and when you're shining, I want you to be on a hill or a lamp stand so that everyone around you will be exposed to the light.

Paul picks up that truth again in Ephesians 5:8 and says to the church, "we walk as children of the light." Everyone who heard those words understood there was nothing more common in their lives than walking. They walked every day just to accomplish the ordinary things

that had to be taken care of in their lives. They understood the implications of Paul's statement. Every day,
in every situation, as you are going through life, shine.
When you're at the market, shine. When you're spending
time at the gate, or drawing water from the well, shine.

Paul also reminded them of who they once were. He
said, "you were once darkness." He didn't say you were
once in darkness; he said you were darkness. He was reminding the Ephesian church that they had previously
been responsible for the spread of darkness. Every room
they had ever entered was exposed to the darkness, every
home they had ever visited, every place they had ever
occupied was exposed to darkness by virtue of their presence. Thankfully, Paul followed that with a reminder that
God's saving grace had made them the exact opposite of
who they once were. He also reminded them of their opportunity to have the opposite effect on the world around
them. No longer would they multiply darkness, but they
would overcome the darkness by walking as children of
the light.

Imagine how encouraged they were to hear Paul's
message. Imagine how empowered they felt to know
that they could impact the darkness of the world around
them. They had a purpose even in the everyday, mun-
dane activities of life, and that purpose was to shine, and
their purpose is our purpose. Paul's encouragement to
the Ephesian church is just as true for us as it was for
them. There is a desperate need for us to walk as children of the light, and we will if we have been changed
by the transforming power of Jesus Christ. We will never
approve of the darkness or the evil activities that hide in
the darkness, but the darkness should motivate us to live

as children of the light. The darker the environment, the greater the need for light. The more invisible Jesus is, the more we shine our light to make Him visible.

We have a reason to be a bright and shining city on a hill. We have a reason to put our light on a lampstand. Lighting the world is our mission. Nobody else can, and nobody else will. It can only happen if every Christian starts living to light up the space around them regardless of how insignificant the space seems to be. According to the 2010 census, there are 2.2 billion Christians worldwide. That means there should be 2.2 billion people lighting up the homes they live in, the workspaces they occupy, the schools they attend, the Church communities they worship with, the streets they walk, and the places they serve. What if that were really happening? Imagine 2.2 billion lights. 2.2 billion people living to make Jesus visible. Imagine 2.2 billion people using their unique ability to communicate Jesus to the people around them. There would be no space, no crevice, no community unexposed to the light of the gospel. That would change the world, and that's what God has called us to do. He wants us to be obvious, not average.

Several years ago, I led a mission's team to serve the homeless on the streets of Philadelphia. Sadly, the city had seen an increase in the number of people living in abandoned buildings, in subway tunnels, and on the streets. Drug abuse was rampant, and many of those trapped by addiction had nowhere else to go. Our plan was clear—we would be staying at the Salvation Army located on Kensington Avenue, we would be using their kitchen facility to prepare about 400 meals, and then we would hit the streets to distribute those meals to the hungry. However, that was only one part of our mission. All of us knew that our biggest reason for being there was to share the love of Jesus with people who were hurting. The men who had signed up for the trip were excited about the opportunity to serve those in need, and our training conversations both equipped and encouraged them to share their faith in the process. Everyone was excited to see our eight-hour trip come to an end. Our youth pastor, Tommy Walton, honked the horn on the van a couple of times, the gate opened, and we pulled into the small parking area located beside the Salvation Army. We had reached our destination, and we couldn't wait to get started. Our first task was to unload the van and the utility trailer, and then settle down for the night.

After a few hours of trying sleep on the uncomfortable concrete floor, we all woke up tired, but ready for a long day of serving Jesus. Like a well-oiled machine, we prepared, cooked, and packaged hundreds of meals. After cleaning up the kitchen, we were finally ready to go out and meet the people we had come to serve. Just before pulling out, we made sure we had the blankets and socks we were going to distribute as well as the hot chocolate and the food. It was all there. "Let's have a word of prayer," I said, and we did. We prayed that God would use us and that people would see Jesus in us. We really wanted that to happen. After a few miles of fighting traffic on Philadelphia's narrow streets, we pulled up to the curb at the corner of Kensington and Somerset and started distributing the meals we had prepared. At first, things were going according to plan; a few people approached our vehicle excited about having a good meal and something warm to drink. Those of us who were volunteering gladly shared what we had available, and we took the time to talk to, and pray with, those who we were serving.

We were doing what we came to do, but that didn't last long. As the crowd grew, our mission seemed to change. We weren't thinking about sharing Jesus anymore, but instead, we were only thinking about giving them food, socks, and blankets. As the day, and even the night went on, we were overwhelmed by people everywhere we stopped. They would rush to our vehicle, and we would hand them the items they wanted as quickly as possible. There was little conversation, virtually no prayer, and a group of good-hearted men who wanted those hurting people to see Jesus. Finally, after a long day of hard work, we reached Love Park located in center city Philadelphia. That was to be our last stop before heading to Jim's for a much-needed late night cheesesteak, but it was what I saw at Love Park that broke my heart.

Just down the street from us, there was a group of college students from Temple University doing exactly what we were doing, feeding the homeless. They weren't there for spiritual reasons at all. Their motivation for being there was college credits. The students explained to me that Temple encourages its students to serve those in need, and rewards them if they do. So, there they were, right beside of us, passing out meals and smiling at each person who took one. There were no conversations about Jesus, no prayers, and no spiritual impact. The only difference between them and us was our desire for people to see and know Jesus, but how was that supposed to happen? At that moment, God crushed me. I realized unsaved people can pass out meals. Unsaved people can smile and be kind. Unsaved people can go out on a cold night and serve hurting people. It became clear to me that we didn't look or sound any different at all to the homeless people who were hurrying to take the meals we were offering. They couldn't mysteriously see Jesus in us. We were dressed in coats, sweaters, gloves, and jeans, just like the college students. We had to open our mouths and make Him known if He was going to be made known.

Why don't we realize that if we fail to talk about Jesus, then we are no different than anyone else? Jesus didn't call us to be social justice crusaders; He called us to be social justice crusaders who share a message. He didn't call us to be just good employees; He called us to be good employees with a message. Jesus didn't call us to be good friends; He called us to be good friends with a message. He didn't call us to be good citizens in our communities; He called us to be good citizens with a message. It is impossible to remove talking about Jesus from the Christian life. It is a must, and I realized it that night standing on the sidewalk at Love Park. I can honestly say that moment changed my life forever, and I left there with a greater awareness of the necessity of talking about Jesus. That is the one thing that allows us to reveal His identity anywhere and at any time. When He is a part of conversations, it informs people that He is a part of our lives. If we don't talk about Jesus, we can't make Him visible. We have to be willing to talk to whomever, whenever, wherever....

PRAYER

God make me more aware of the people that You put in my path, and give me the courage to share the gospel with a greater boldness than I ever have before. Give me a greater confidence in the saving power of the gospel so I will trust the gospel and not my ability to share it. Give me the wisdom to know the difference between compelling people to come to Christ, and attempting to coerce people to come to Christ. Make my light shine brighter than it ever has before so more people will see Jesus through me. In Jesus' name, Amen!

REFLECT

1. Ephesians 2:10 says we are God's workmanship, created in Christ for good works. We are creation— He is Creator. What good works is God producing in you?

2. When was the last time, or who was the last person you talked to about Jesus? List the names of five people, in your sphere of influence, that you really should talk to:

3. Peter cursed by the fireside in an attempt to lead people to believe he wasn't a follower of Jesus — List some of the specific ways you camouflage your faith in Jesus when you are at work, school, or with friends?

4. How closely aligned is your life with 2 Peter 1:5–8?

5. What is your most heartbreaking missed opportunity? You should have made Jesus visible and you didn't....

"So relational evangelism? Go for it, as long as it turns into real evangelism. You hanging out having a beer with your buddy so he can see that Christians are cool is not what we're called to do. You're eventually going to have to open up your mouth and share the gospel. When the pure gospel is shared, people respond."

Matt Chandler

CHAPTER 4

HIS LOVE FOR US, OUR LOVE FOR HIM, AND OUR LOVE FOR OTHERS

W e've all heard the old saying, "the best advertisement is word of mouth." And it's true! Personal testimony has a level of believability and credibility that cannot be matched by any other means of advertisement or promotion. No savvy marketing campaign, no product sales pitch, no media strategy can equal the power of people personally representing a product or a place. When a friend says to another friend, "You have to taste this," "You have to see this place," or "You have to wear these clothes," it virtually ensures that you will eat at that restaurant, visit that vacation destination, or shop at that clothing store. That's what makes popular places popular. Repeated endorsements by ordinary people create the popular trends. The word on the street makes a difference. It's not the owner or the distributor personally encountering every single individual, but it's you and I becoming personal representatives of a specific place or product. Knowing that truth is eye-opening because it makes us aware of the fact that we are all evangelists. We practice evangelism every single day. We evangelize for the local cupcake bakery, the local coffee shop, the new barbecue restaurant, the accountant who prepared our taxes, the outlet center that saved us money, and through our evangelistic efforts, people are reached for the businesses we represent in our everyday conversations. That means we are already naturally doing what Jesus has asked us to do. The problem is, we're not doing it for Him!

Why are we more willing to be a representative for our favorite restaurant than we are for Jesus? Why are we more excited about the latest fashion trends than we are about Jesus? Why are we more willing to put ourselves out there for a vacation destination than we are for Jesus? Those are bold questions that demand an honest answer. Is it that we don't truly believe Jesus' words in Matthew 10:33, "but whoever denies me before men, I also will deny before my Father who is in heaven"? Can you imagine hearing the crucified Christ say the words, "Father I don't know them," or "they never lived as if they knew me." That is almost too painful even to imagine. The thought of hearing those words creates in me a healthy fear of Jesus' power and authority. It makes me feel as if I need to fall on my face afresh and pray with conviction, "God never let those words be spoken over me!" Please, never let me be ashamed of the gospel, or the Christ of the gospel!

My heart's cry is increasingly becoming, "Jesus, be visible in my life." More and more often I am living with an awareness of the tension that the gospel generates inside of me. Divine discomfort is causing me to live with chronic spiritual pain because of the weakness of my flesh and my propensity to apathy. Frequently I am wrestling with the questions, how could I be ashamed of Jesus anywhere or with anyone? How could I be ashamed of the One who was put to an open shame for me? I know these questions are uncomfortable, but all of us have a spiritual obligation to acknowledge the cause of our shame. All of us need to have a personal confrontation with the reality that we rarely live to make Jesus visible.

We can't dodge the fact that we are not representing Him well in the spaces we occupy. Oh, it's easy for us to talk about the Super Bowl, or our most recent adventure, or the gift we were given on our special occasion. We want to make sure that our family and friends know about the home we recently moved into or the new car we just purchased. It's easy to invite our acquaintances to our child's birthday celebration, or our backyard cookout. It's just not easy for us to publicly own our relationship with Jesus, and yet that is exactly what Jesus calls us to do. There is no alternate Christian life that does not include broadcasting the news of Jesus.

> That which was from the beginning, which we
> have heard, which we have seen with our eyes,
> which we looked upon and have touched with
> our hands, concerning the word of life—the
> life was made manifest, and we have seen it,
> and testify to it and proclaim to you the eternal

life, which was with the Father and was made
manifest to us—that which we have seen and
heard we proclaim also to you, so that you too
may have fellowship with us; and indeed our
fellowship is with the Father and with his Son
Jesus Christ. And we are writing these things
so that our joy may be complete. This is the
message we have heard from him and proclaim
to you, that God is light, and in him is no darkness at all. If we say we have fellowship with
him while we walk in darkness, we lie and do
not practice the truth. But if we walk in the
light, as he is in the light, we have fellowship
with one another, and the blood of Jesus his
Son cleanses us from all sin.

(1 John 1:1–7)

It is impossible to encounter Jesus and not talk about
Jesus. If He has revealed Himself to you, you can't help
but reveal Him to others. The Apostle John's conversations were entirely changed as a result of encountering
Jesus. He wanted to share the news of eternal life. He
wanted everyone He came in contact with to experience
community with Jesus and with other believers. Sharing
that message was his greatest joy! Representing Jesus was
his highest honor. That was the result of being purified
by the shed blood of Jesus. That was the result of walking
with Jesus in the light. J.D. Greear quoted the words of
Charles Spurgeon in his book *Jesus Continued*,

If Jesus is precious to you (as he is to the
Spirit), you will not be able to keep your good

news to yourself; you will be whispering it in your child's ear; you will be telling it to your husband; you will be earnestly imparting it to your friend; without the charms of eloquence you will be more than eloquent; your heart will speak, and your eyes will flash as you talk of his sweet love....It cannot be that there is a high appreciation of Jesus and a totally silent tongue.

I read that, and I wonder how many people's failure to make Jesus visible is proof that they have never truly had an encounter with Jesus? A person can't represent Him if he or she isn't a representative of Him.

We know the scripture teaches that it is possible to have an intellectual knowledge of Jesus, but no experiential knowledge of Jesus. Like the demons mentioned in James 2:19, there are people who believe that He is the Son of God, but they have never really believed in Him as the Savior of their soul, and the Lord over their life. Remember, Jesus can't be visible through us until He is first visible to us. The only thing that would ever create a desire in us to make Jesus known is salvation, and if as you're reading these words, you're feeling convicted about whether or not you have truly been saved, please stop reading right now and experience the Jesus who is making Himself visible to you.

Thankfully, God's grace is available for the religiously lost just as much as it is for the recklessly lost. He still has the power to cry out, "come forth" to those who are dead in their sins and resurrect them to new life. His cross redeems the confused. His love reaches the falsely convinced. His Spirit searches out those who are sitting in the pews attempting to achieve salvation. If that is you, respond now! Matthew Henry gave this commentary on 2 Corinthians 6:2, "The gospel day is a day of salvation, the means of grace the means of salvation, the offers of the gospel the offers of salvation, and the present time the proper time to accept these offers." That couldn't possibly be said any better, and if you feel God speaking to your heart about the condition of your soul that is grace, and the proper time to respond to grace is always immediately.

Our failure to make Jesus visible can also be an issue of our love for Jesus. It's not that we don't love Jesus at all—we just don't love Him most. Because when we love Him most, we will make Him most visible. I witnessed this being true a few years ago in the life of my precious friend, Jack Faughn. For several years Jack lived as a single adult, lonely and longing for love. His conversations were often tearful, and his desire to be married was evident. Finally, God's answer to Jack's prayers was introduced to him. Her name was Megan. She was a beautiful, outgoing, godly young lady from Arkansas. After a few months of long conversations, dating, and growing to love one another, it was clear that Megan felt just as strongly about Jack as he felt about her. On May 30, 2015, I had the opportunity to invite them to turn and face an audience and introduce them as husband and wife. They walked off the platform that day hand in hand, and I'm honestly not sure they've let go for more than a moment since then.

Recently, I had the opportunity to watch Jack and Megan interact with other people, and as I watched, I noticed a simple, but beautiful expression of love. Jack was introducing Megan to everyone. The moment someone would engage Jack in a conversation, he would politely interrupt and say, "This is my wife, Megan." That small gesture communicated to every single person who was privileged to hear those words that Jack is proud of his wife, he doesn't want her to go unnoticed. I'm confident that he never introduced her to anyone that day without enjoying hearing himself say the words, "This is my wife." Jack's recognition of Megan was indicative of his feelings for her.

When you truly love someone; you don't want them to go unnoticed or unacknowledged. You don't mind interrupting the moment to ask, "Have you met...?" Or "Have I introduced you to...?" It's an expression of love or respect. It says to the person you're talking to, "There is someone with me who is more important than me at this moment." There is someone with me that I won't allow to remain nameless. There is someone I would like for you to meet. Our serious issue is, rarely is that person Jesus. We say we love Him, and yet we rarely take a moment to introduce Him to the people we meet. We have conversation after conversation without ever asking anyone the question, "Have I introduced you to Jesus?" He's like that person we call our friend, but in reality, he or she is more like our "friend." It's more of a private friendship. We're nice because we wouldn't want to hurt his or her feelings, but that is as far as it goes. Being in public with "them" would be uncomfortable. We might feel a little embarrassed or fearful about our reputation.

We may not want to admit it, but at some point in time, we have treated someone like that or been treated like that by someone. We don't like it, we certainly don't like being on the receiving end of it, but sadly, we're willing to make Jesus the recipient of that treatment far too often. He stays in the car while we go into the restaurant for dinner. He is confined to the basement while we hang out with friends in the living room. He stays at home while we go on vacation. That seems to be what we think is happening, but that's not what's going on at all. In Matthew 28:20, He promised to be with us always. That means He's with us every single time we act like He's not. He's right there with us every time we fail to introduce Him, or every time we would be embarrassed to be identified with Him. He's there every time we avoid bringing Him into the conversation and every time we hide our relationship with Him by going along with the crowd.

It seems like an evangelism issue, doesn't it? Maybe the church should introduce a new and improved evangelism training resource, or maybe the church should teach some better, more efficient evangelism strategies. The church could, and even has, but evangelism isn't the actual problem. It's a love issue. The truth is, you can't disconnect John 14:15 and Matthew 28:19. Jesus said, "If you love me keep my commands," and He clearly commanded, "therefore go and make disciples of all nations." Making disciples is an issue of loving Jesus. We don't introduce Jesus because we don't love Him enough to force His introduction into the conversation. We want Him to know that we know Him, that means we receive all the luxuries and benefits of heaven, but we don't want the people around us to know that we know Him, because that means we receive all the rejection and ridicule. To display Him in the storefront window of our conversations would be too embarrassing. It's not that we don't want Jesus to be visible, saying that would be too harsh, we just want someone else to introduce Him. Our excuses are we just don't know enough to start that conversation, or we're just too introverted, or we're not as skilled with the Bible as we need to be, but the truth is, we just don't love Him enough to make Him visible.

Do you know who we introduce most often? Ourselves! Toby Keith sang the truth in his country song, "I Wanna Talk About Me." The lyrics are spot on, "I wanna talk about me, wanna talk about I, wanna talk about number one, oh my me my, what I think, what I like, what I know, what I want, what I see." That describes us. We talk about who we are, where we've been, and what we've done, or what we have to do. We talk about our families, our children, our interests, our hobbies, our dreams, and our pains. We continuously introduce and reintroduce ourselves over and over again, but why? The answer is in Luke 6:45. Jesus taught, "for out of the abundance of the heart the mouth speaks." A few chapters later in Luke 12:34, He said, "for where your treasure is, there will your heart be also." Jesus taught with great clarity that a person's heart is their own personal treasure chest.

Our hearts hold what we value most. The people, things, thoughts, and pleasures that we cherish all find a place of priority in our hearts. Jesus also taught with great clarity that what fills our hearts eventually exits our mouths. Our conversations betray us; they reveal who we really are, and they showcase what we truly care about. Our tongues won't allow us to hide our passions, feelings, loves, and emotions. There is no squelch setting on our hearts capable of suppressing the constant feedback of our self-promotion. It's really not that difficult to identify. If we would just listen intently to the everyday conversations that take place around us, we would hear it. If we dissected our own conversations phrase by phrase, we would realize that the majority of our conversations are typically focused on the person we love most, which is our self. That means the key to us being better representatives of Jesus is loving Him more than we love ourselves and more than we love all the meaningless things that dominate our conversations. It means loving Him first above anything and everything else.

In Revelation 3:20, the Church in Laodicea had allowed their hearts to become overcrowded. That's why Jesus said He was knocking on their heart's door. He was supposed to be inside. He was supposed to be preeminent in their hearts and be their foremost affection, but instead, He was on the wrong side of the threshold, pleading with them to open the door. It wasn't that the Laodicean Church had lost all their affection for Jesus, but it was an issue of overcrowding created by misappropriated affection. The Laodicean Church was just like the overcrowded inn in Luke 2:7. Jesus wasn't excluded from the inn because the innkeeper was a bigot who looked down on Joseph and Mary. Unlike the Church's portrayal of the innkeeper in the annual Christmas play, the Bible never says that the innkeeper said the words, "there is no room in the inn." He wasn't a raving lunatic, and the words "you can't stay here" weren't shouted at the struggling newlyweds from Nazareth. He allowed Joseph and Mary to occupy the only space he had available. It just so happened that space was outside. That's where Jesus was born, in the stable that night in Bethlehem. His birth took place there because there was no room for Him in the

inn. The population of Bethlehem had increased exponentially due to the tax mandate, and by the time Joseph
and Mary arrived, the inn was already overcrowded. That
meant Jesus would be given what was left, and what was
left was a dirty, unpleasant stable.

Something inside of me cringes each time I stop and
think that Jesus was born in a stable. As a father of three, I
can't imagine even one of my children being born in those
filthy conditions. How could Jesus be denied a place in
the inn? How could the King of Kings and Lord of Lords
be born surrounded by animals? Those are all legitimate
questions, and they are exactly the questions I ask when
I read Revelation 3:20. How could the Laodicean Christians place so little value on Jesus? Why wasn't their relationship with Him more significant to them? How could
they allow Jesus to be pushed outside of the church?
These are the kind of condescending questions that flood
my mind, and I would love to ask the Laodicean Church
when I read those verses. It's way too easy for me to rise
up in judgment and say, "How dare they display the no
vacancy sign on their heart's door?" or "How dare they
ignore Jesus!" Because intellectually I believe that Jesus
should never have to knock on the door of a Christian's
heart, ever!

Jesus should be appreciated, honored, and adored.
That is what I say I believe, but my reaction to Luke 2 and
Revelation 3, in all honesty, is hypocritical. The truth is,
I am guilty of doing the exact same thing. You see, I have
an inn and a stable in my life. The inn is my best—the
stable is what I have left. The inn is where I place all the
things that matter most to me—the stable is where the
less important things end up once the inn is full. The inn

is where Jesus should be; the stable is where He is often found. The truth is, I allow my own heart to become so overcrowded with meaningless things. Instead of Jesus being held as my greatest treasure, my heart becomes a trophy case filled to capacity with all the trophies I've awarded myself. Each one of them is nothing more than a shiny testament to my pride. Each one of them is engraved with my accomplishments, achievements, and desires. That is why when I open my mouth, I most often tell the story of me. That is why you most often tell the story of you.

Our mouths are the gateways that allow our heart's passions to make their grand entrance into the world around us. So, making Jesus visible is actually a heart issue. It's a love issue. You and I will never live to make Jesus visible until we love Him most. He doesn't influence our conversations from the stable. He will never direct our actions from outside of the inn. His presence doesn't fill our hearts until we love Him most, and it's when we love Him most that His identity matters most. He will never be first in our conversations until He is first in our hearts and lives. How often we talk about Him is ultimately determined by how much we love Him. If you examine your heart right now in light of that truth, where is He in your life? Is He in the inn or is He in the stable? Is He your first love or is He an afterthought? Do you find yourself frequently saying, "have I ever introduced you to Jesus?" or does he rarely enter your conversations? Is He included when you share your life's story, or do you skip that part? Your answers to these questions will be a strong indicator of how deeply in love with Jesus you really are, and I pray we are honest enough to be convicted about our need to love Him more.

We are who we are because of Jesus' love for us, and we become who He has called us to be because of our love for Him. 1 John 3:1 is true. "See what kind of love the Father has given to us [lavished on us), that we should be called the children of God." 1 John 4:19 says, "We love Him because He first loved us." Please embrace the truth in these verses! Everything we are, we owe to outrageous, unconditional, incomprehensible love of God. Neither you nor I have earned our place in God's family. We are His children by divine providence. We were dead, and He raised us to life. We were without faith and grace, and He gave us both faith and grace (Ephesians 2:8-9). None of us have a salvation story that includes the words, "Let me tell you what I did." We did nothing—Jesus did everything. The song of salvation will forever, eternally be, "You were slain, and by your blood you ransomed people for God from every tribe and language and people and nation" (Revelation 5:9). "Worthy is the Lamb, who was slain, to receive wealth and honor and glory and praise (Revelation 5:12)!" Notice the "I" is silent in both of those verses. No one crying out, "I was worthy to be slain—I redeemed myself." Heaven will never hear anyone sing that song because none of us were, are, or ever will be worthy to redeem ourselves. Our redemption is based solely on Jesus' love for us. We were unlovable, undeserving of love, but that didn't stop Him from loving us anyway. That didn't prevent Him from demonstrating a love for us that is beyond anything we have ever known. The "anyway" love of God is immeasurable, and unfathomable, but "anyway" love is the great love that has been bestowed on us!

It's because of His love that the words of 2 Corinthians 5:17, "Therefore, if anyone is in Christ, he is a new creation. The old has passed away; behold, the new has come" are true for us. What an awesome reality! Jesus loved us enough to be willing to make us new creations. We can all say who I was, is not who I am, and who I am is not who I am becoming. That is incredible! We haven't been refurbished; we've been remade. We're not a better version of our former selves; we are entirely new creations. That is worth celebrating! That deserves awe and amazement! To think that through the power of the sinless life of Christ, the sacrificial death of Christ, and the supernatural resurrection of Christ, we are new creations in Him. I love to hear Big Daddy Weave sing the words, "I don't have to be the old man inside of me, his day is long dead and gone, I've got a new name, a new life, I'm not the same, and a hope that will carry me home, I am redeemed." The words, "we are a new creation" are overwhelmingly exciting, but the verse doesn't end with those words. God's work in our lives doesn't end there either. He doesn't make us new just to make us new; He makes us new so that we can live for a new purpose.

2 Corinthians 5:18 introduces us to a unique gift from God. It's not a gift to just be celebrated; it's a gift to be operated. Don't misunderstand, it is a gift, but it's a gift that comes with an enormous responsibility. No one is excluded—no one is excused—no one is exempted—everyone gets the gift. Everyone who experiences 2 Corinthians 5:17 also experiences 2 Corinthians 5:18. The "anyone" in verse 17 is the "us" in verse 18, and every-

one who is made a new creation in Christ is given the ministry of reconciliation. The ministry of announcing to people that through Jesus, they can be reconciled to God. It's word-of-mouth advertising. It's saying to a world that's far away from God, "you don't have to be far away from God." It's making sure the people around you know the truth of 2 Corinthians 5:21: For our sake he (God) made him (Jesus) to be sin who knew no sin, so that in him (Jesus) we might become the righteousness of God. That is the most beautiful love story the world has ever known. The story of a God who loved sinful people so much that He was willing to give His own son's life to rescue them. The story of a son who was willing to shed His divine glory and live among the people He created as a penniless outcast. The story of the son allowing Himself to be rejected, abused, beaten, and crucified, so that He could make those sinful people a part of God's family. That is the greatest story ever told, and we get to share it. We have the joy of letting people know that the unconditional love of Jesus is available. That is the incredible ministry that God has given to us.

When we stop and realize just how extravagant Jesus' love is, it increases our desire to make His love known to the world around us. 2 Corinthians 5:19 cannot be confined to the shadows of our conversations or imprisoned in our hearts. Our desire to see people reconciled to God motivates us to share all that we have experienced in Christ. We want them to know, "In Christ God was reconciling the world to Himself, not counting their trespasses against them." We want them to know that God has provided a way for their broken relationship with Him to be mended. Yes, we are the ones who failed God, but God is the one who has made a way for us to be reconciled. We want people to encounter that incredible truth. Warren Wiersbe ascribed all the credit to Jesus for the miracle of reconciliation when he wrote the words, "The Person who reconciles us to God is Jesus Christ, and the place where He reconciles us is His cross." Yes, the cross was bloody, but that truth makes the cross stunningly beautiful. It was on the cross that Jesus restored the broken relationship between God and man. The Roman soldiers didn't know when they nailed His hands to the cross that He was reaching out to God with one hand, and reaching out to fallen man with the other. They didn't know when they spread His arms wide open that He was saying to a hopeless world, "I love you this much." They didn't realize the story of the gospel would be the story of the outrageous love of God for sinful people, but that is the story that's repeated each time the gospel is shared.

Every person who shares the gospel shares the story of a love so great that it caused God to call out to a lost world through His crucified son, "come to me." Each person who talks out the story of a love so rich that it would allow fallen people the privilege of complete, absolute forgiveness. A forgiveness that is so amazing it exceeds our past. It's the story of our sins being laid on Jesus, and in turn, His righteousness being laid on us. That is the greatest exchange the world has ever known, and we have the privilege of sharing the story of God's unfair grace. It was entirely unfair that Jesus took our sin, our shame, and our hell, and in return, gave us His righteousness, His honor, and His peace. It was unfair that God turned His back on Jesus so He could turn His face toward us. How could we not want to share that story with the world? 2 Corinthians 5:19 says it is "the message of reconciliation." That is our message, and every believer has been called to share it. Every believer should say at some point in the conversation, "Let me tell you what Jesus has done for me." That conversation emerges from a place of gratitude for the grace and goodness that God has extended to us. In addition to His grace and goodness, Jesus has saved us and equipped us with a message. He has also commissioned us to share that message and make Him visible to the world around us.

2 Corinthians 5:20 says, "Therefore, we are ambassadors for Christ"—which means we are accredited diplomats sent by Him as His official representatives. The preposition "for" in the text implies that we are acting on Christ's behalf. We are Christ's representatives sent to negotiate with people on His behalf regarding the issue of reconciliation. The ministry of reconciliation is our official business. The message of reconciliation is our official message. The work of reconciliation is our official work. Christians are the only representatives of Jesus on the planet with the message of the cross committed to the work of Christ. If we don't represent Jesus in the world, no one will. That demands that we deal with every personal issue that keeps us from making Jesus visible. Even the issues that are not a matter of sin, but still have the power to diminish our spiritual effectiveness. Virtually all of us know those common issues, but we still allow them to keep us from boldly representing Jesus.

The most common issue seems to be fear. Almost everyone experiences fear when they try to introduce Jesus into the conversation. There is the fear of publicly owning your faith—the fear of people's opinion of you—and certainly the fear of rejection. All those are outward expressions of our inward fear. They are undeniable, and the effects are evident. 1 John 4:18 says that "fear has torment," and if we allow it, tormenting fear can paralyze us. Rick Warren said, "Fear is a self-imposed prison that will keep you from becoming what God intends for you to be." That is unquestionably true when it comes to being an effective witness. It takes courage and breaking out of our self-imposed prisons. Fear cannot be allowed to dictate where we make Jesus visible and to whom we make Jesus visible.

R.A. Torrey said in his book, *Power-Filled Living*, "When Christians answer the call to work in God's harvest field, they may be sent across the street to witness to a neighbor or across the ocean to a different culture... prepare your heart and testify about the Lord Jesus." R.A. Torrey's advice, "prepare your heart," is great advice given in acknowledgment of the fact that it takes a prepared resolve to witness for Jesus. If we wait until we're in the moment to try and muster up enough courage, there is a good possibility fear will win, but it doesn't have to. God will give us the strength to share His story with the person across the table, the person across the street, the person across the world, or even the person right in front of us. Sometimes, it may seem that across the street is more challenging than across the world, but the more you completely depend on Him, the easier it will be to say the words, "let me tell you about Jesus."

Another common problem that many people face is the feeling of being unworthy or unqualified to share Jesus with anyone. People frequently say things like, "I'm not a good enough Christian," or "I just don't know enough."

What they're actually expressing when they make those statements is their doubt in God's ability to use them. People who feel unworthy don't understand the fullness of Christ's saving work in their lives. They don't understand that it isn't their strength that empowers the gospel, but rather God's strength. It's easy for them to see God, in Christ, pleading with people to be saved. Through each miracle, through each sermon, through each act of compassion, and ultimately through Jesus' death, God was reaching out to the world and drawing people to Himself. Every Christian can see that—but it's much more difficult for a lot of Christians to fully understand how God could now be making His appeal to the world through us (2 Corinthians 5:20).

Those words carry such enormous weight. When Jesus was on the earth, God was reaching out to the world through Him, but now that Jesus is no longer on the earth, God is reaching out to the world through you and me. It's through our lives, our conversations, our characteristics, and our displays of grace that God is saying to the world around us, "you need Me." He is doing that through us now because we are here in Jesus' place. Now that He is gone, He relies on His ambassadors to share His heart with the world. Whether He is visible or invisible in the spaces we occupy depends on whether or not we live to represent Him well. Whether people know God's love story or not depends on whether or not we share it. A great question to ask yourself is this, "Had Jesus represented God in the same way I represent Jesus, how many people would know about God?"

2 Corinthians 4:3 is one of the most challenging verses in all the Bible. It is a strong reminder of a convicting

truth that we would really rather ignore. The Christian life would be so much more convenient if the reality of this one verse didn't exist. In the King James Version, it reads, "if our gospel be hid, it is hid to them that are lost." Every time I read those words, they leave me feeling heavy-hearted. They bring me face-to-face with my failure. I don't want to admit that I am guilty of hiding the gospel. I even ask myself, "How could I do something so horrible?" The gospel is the power of God to salvation, and salvation is what the world needs to escape hell, so what would make me hide it? I ask myself that question, and immediately, my deceitful heart looks for a way to avoid the truth. My heart says, "Brian, you do share the gospel, every time you preach you point people to the gospel." My evasive response is "Yeah that's right, I do. I talk about the gospel, I pray and give thanks for the gospel, I even sing about the gospel. So yes, I'm sure there are people out there who may hide the gospel, but not me." Then I hear God's Spirit speak over the self-reassuring pride of my heart, and it's when He calls me to examine Paul's statement that I have to confess, "Yes, I do hide the gospel." Paul's statement will likely lead you to confess that you are guilty of hiding the gospel as well. It doesn't happen because we hate the gospel, but it happens because we are hypocritical with the gospel.

My dear friend, Pastor Jon Bowman, said in a recent conversation, "You aren't being courageous with the gospel until you share it in places you don't belong, places where you don't fit in, and places where it isn't appreciated. That's when you're being courageous."

That is the issue; it's easier to be hypocritical than it is to be courageous. We have no problem loving and celebrating the gospel when we're with other people who love and celebrate the gospel. It's easy to sing the words, "Hallelujah, death is beaten Christ has risen from the grave, Hallelujah, it is finished all to Him the highest praise" when we are in a crowd of people who are singing along. It's easy for us to nod in agreement with the message of the gospel when we're sitting in a church building with other like-minded believers. It's easy to have gospel conversations and use all the latest gospel clichés when we're talking to other Christians, but Paul didn't say in his Corinthian letter that the gospel was being hidden by believers when they were in the company of other believers. That's not who we hide the gospel from. We hide the gospel from the people who are lost.

Our boldness intensifies or diminishes as our crowd changes. We are courageous when we are with other Christians and cowards when we are with the lost. This means we are hypocritical with the gospel. We are selective when it comes to who we display the gospel to and who we hide it from. The sad thing is, we allow the gospel to shine where it's taken for granted, and we allow it to be hidden where it's most needed. The people who are lost are the very ones who need to see the gospel. British evangelist Gypsy Smith once said in a sermon, "There are five gospels—Matthew, Mark, Luke, John, and the Christian, but most people may never read the first four." While I appreciate the power of this great statement, I can't help but think that most people will have a far better chance of encountering the four gospels. Each of them is displayed on pages for the world to see, but too often the fifth one is intentionally hidden so that no one sees. The heartbreaking truth is, it's being hidden from the people who are lost.

Stop and think about what it means to be lost. Think about all the consequences of living and dying without Jesus. The truth is, rarely do we stop and think about that. Day after day, we interact with people, and never once do we see them as Jesus did in Mark 6:34, as sheep without a shepherd. We don't think about it. When we're hurrying down the street or rushing through the department store, we just don't think about the fact that we are surrounded by people who are lost. I know it is an unpleasant reality. I know that fewer and fewer people have that conversation, and more and more pastors avoid that subject all together.

However, our silence doesn't change the fact that there are multitudes of people without God. They are God's creation, but they are not God's children. They have never received Him, and therefore, they have never been given the power to become the children of God (John 1:12). That means that every present and eternal benefit given exclusively to God's children doesn't belong to them and that every present and eternal consequence does. The thought of that breaks my heart. I shouldn't view anything as being sadder than a person living and dying without Jesus. The words of 2 Thessalonians 1:8–10 proves there is nothing sadder,

> in flaming fire, inflicting vengeance on those who do not know God and on those who do not obey the gospel of our Lord Jesus. They will suffer the punishment of eternal destruction, away from the presence of the Lord and

from the glory of his might, when he comes
on that day to be glorified in his saints, and to
be marveled at among all who have believed,
because our testimony to you was believed."

That is why we can't hide the gospel. That is why we
have to make Jesus visible to those who are lost.

PRAYER

God, please help me to be courageous with the gospel. Strengthen me to represent Jesus well. Help me to overcome my fears. Burden me to share the gospel with my family, friends, neighbors, and co-workers. Give me a fresh awareness of what it means to be lost, and may that awareness drive me to my knees. You've entrusted me with the message of the gospel, and I pray that it would never be hidden in my life. In Jesus' name, Amen.

REFLECT

1. Describe the impact Matthew 10:33 has on you when you read it in light of your life:

2. Why do we believe we can lay claim to salvation without ever making Jesus visible, when there is no scriptural basis for that salvation?

3. Does Jesus live in your inn or your stable? What are you often guilty of loving more than you love Him?

4. The gospel transforms people's lives—how has it transformed yours? With your bible opened to 2 Corinthians 5:17, write out the story of your encounter with the gospel and the results of that encounter:

5. How are you currently representing gospel reconciliation in our divided culture?

"Every Christian is either a missionary or an imposter"

Charles Spurgeon

CHAPTER 5:

JESUS HAS TO BE BIGGER TO YOU THAN YOU

Several years ago, I heard a story about a little girl who couldn't quite understand what she had heard during her pastor's sermon one Sunday morning. She had listened closely, but that wasn't the problem. The problem was this one statement he had made just didn't make sense to her. The sermon that day had been centered around the greatness of God, and over and over again the pastor had repeated the statement, "we serve a big God!" That wasn't what confused her. She believed that God was big. She had heard that taught in Sunday school. The statement that had her confused was, "this really big God wants to make your heart His home." How is that possible, she wondered? How can such a big God live inside of me? She wanted to know the answers to her questions.

Finally, her family finished talking to all their friends and made the familiar walk from the church building to their car. She waited anxiously for a moment while they drove away from the church building and then she slid forward in her seat and said, "Mom and Dad, I have a question," to which the mom and dad responded, "Okay, sweetie, ask away." She continued, "the pastor said today that God is so big that He created the Earth, and measured all the waters in His hand and put all the stars and the planets in the sky exactly where they belonged, is that true?" The mom and dad answered, "Yes, darling it is true, He did all those things." She continued, "but then the pastor said that God wants to live in our hearts, is that true?" Again, the dad and mom answered, "yes darling, that is true also." The inquisitive little girl went silent for a few minutes while she thought about what she had just heard. Finally, after her brief pause was over, she slid forward in her seat again, and asked one final question, "well, Mom and Dad, if God is really big, and He lives in our hearts, won't He stick out?" She may have been small, but she had asked a giant question, and the answer to her giant question was, and is, yes, He will. If the all-powerful, almighty God of the universe lives in us, He will stick out.

We are designed to celebrate, express, and reveal the things that are big to us. It happens every day all around us. Sports fans proudly wear the logo of their favorite team on a shirt or a hat. Motorcycle enthusiasts have an entire wardrobe bearing the brand name of the bike they ride. Our homes are decorated with the pictures of our children and grandchildren. Our car's bumper or rear window is often covered with stickers announcing to other motorists where we like to vacation or which candidate has our political support. Without any verbal interaction at all, we are still communicating what is important to us. View a person's Facebook page or Instagram posts for just a few days, and you will know what they are into or what they care about most. Every day, in a multitude of ways, we announce to the people around us, "this is what I care about, this is what is big in my life." That announcement should reveal Jesus. It will reveal Jesus if He is bigger to us than everything and everyone else. We can't keep that from happening. The bigger He is to us, the more He will stick out in our lives. The more significant He becomes in our life, the more significant He becomes through our life. That is why we can't overlook the importance of having a right perspective on how big He is, and how small we are.

Colossians 1:18 is more than a verse; it's a lifestyle. The words "that in all things He might be preeminent" make more than a statement; those words should shape the way we live our lives. Those words call us to settle in our hearts, once and for all, that Jesus is to be preeminent, not in some things, but in all things. Jesus is to be preeminent in our conversations and our actions. He is to be preeminent in our characteristics and our decisions. He is to be preeminent in our marriages and our parenting. Jesus is even to be preeminent in our finances. This list could go on and on because, in every identifiable area of life, Jesus is to be preeminent. Living in that way is ultimately living a life of worship. All that you are bows in submission to all that He is. That cannot happen if there is any resistance in you regarding the fact that you are inferior to Him. Your will doesn't matter as much as His will; your identity doesn't matter as much as His identity. Your autonomy is lost in the vast expanse of His authority. "God is greater" is no longer just a statement you sing in a worship song, but God's greatness and superiority is the banner that waves over your life.

Very few Christians seem to understand that salvation may involve prayer, but salvation is not in a prayer. Salvation may be called a good decision, but salvation is not just a good decision. Biblical salvation is described as a transfer of ownership. 1 Corinthians 6:20 says to every Christian everywhere, "you are not your own." Johann Bengel wrote, "you are entirely in the power of another." This transaction happens the moment we are saved. The deed to our life is no longer in our possession, and our full authority is relinquished. It's much like the home my family currently lives in. The previous owners no longer have the right to decorate the interior of our home or alter the exterior at all. The color of the paint or the arrangement of the furniture is not their decision to make. They don't even have the legal right to enter our home uninvited, and in the six years we've lived, there they have never once tried. It doesn't matter that they originally designed and built that specific house. They are not the current owners, and never once have either of them acted like they were supposed to have any continuing authority over the house. That's because they walked away from the closing with a full understanding that the deed was no longer in their possession.

That same thing is true for the person who crosses the line of faith and receives Jesus' forgiveness, Jesus' righteousness, and Jesus' payment for sin. Ownership is transferred through that divine transaction. Realizing that truth is invaluable. Completely owning the fact that He owns me puts me in my rightful place of worshipper and Him in His rightful place of preeminence. When you and I grasp that, the result is a paradigm shift that doesn't just change the way we live but changes why we live.

The resounding confession of our heart becomes, "God is greater than I am, His will for my life is greater than my will for my life, His identity is greater than my identity." Viewing life from that perspective is necessary for everyone who has a desire to make Jesus visible. We want nothing more than to be small so that our really big God will stick out.

1 Corinthians 6:20 doesn't stop with the words, "you are not your own." It would still be incredibly strong if it did, but it goes on to say, "you were bought with a price." What a humbling statement, and even more so, what a humbling thought. Talk about putting things into perspective. Just take a moment to marinate in the depths of the confrontational truth: I am God's property. I am not my own person, and I don't have authority over my life. Saying that sounds strange. We have all heard over and over again, "Be your own person," and "Choose what you want to do with your own life." But the Christian's song is, "Jesus paid it all, all to Him I owe." It has to be. A Christian is a Christian because he or she has been bought and paid for by God. Not with gold or silver, but with the sinless blood of Jesus (1 Peter 1:18–19).

The God who could claim ownership of us because He created us instead paid for us as if we deserved to be bought and not just discarded. The God who could have demanded by virtue of His omnipotence that we live indebted to Him instead paid the ultimate price for us as if we were a treasure to be desired. In the most supreme act of benevolence ever known in all human history, God exceeded every requirement necessary to make unworthy sinners His children. Seeing God in His rightful place of ownership allows me to see myself in my rightful place as His servant. It affirms in me that He is great and I am not.

John 3:30 is only seven words. "He must increase, but I must decrease." It's one simple sentence, and yet, that is all it took for John the Baptist to establish both Jesus' and our rightful place. He spoke these words so plainly that the meaning is unmistakable. There is no digging deeper into the original language or studying each word in detail searching for a hidden meaning. Simply read the verse, and you know where you belong and where Jesus belongs. You would have to close your eyes or look away to miss John's instruction. Jesus belongs in the forefront, and we belong in the background; Jesus belongs in the spotlight, and we belong behind the curtain; Jesus belongs on the throne, and we belong on our faces, bowing in humility before Him. He is to be perpetually increasing in importance in our lives, and we are to be perpetually decreasing.

That is what I say I believe. Most of us would likely say that is what we believe. Yes, Jesus deserves all the honor, all the glory, and all the attention. Yet, if we are honest, rarely does that become anything more than an ideology. There is no real sense of urgency in us regarding the discrepancy that exists between our way of living and John 3:30. Think about it. How often do we start our day by praying, "God, please help me to decrease." The truthful answer is either never, or very rarely, because we don't think like that. We don't live lives focused on decreasing. If we're honest, we think more as Nebuchadnezzar did in the first two chapters in the book of Daniel. We are consumed with our own dreams, and we attempt to use the people in our lives to advance them. We obsess over what we want to accomplish and what we want to fulfill or what we need to be fulfilled. Unlike Nebuchadnezzar, we have no plans to build a massive statue in our honor, but we are the greatest cause in our own minds.

Christians have ingested the false gospel of prosperity and the culture's false gospel of humanism until it has poisoned our view of God's grace, goodness, and glory. The theme of so many sermon series and current Christian books is, you can increase, you deserve it, and God owes it to you. That false message has become an acceptable, even celebrated gospel. Pastors in American churches have congregations ignoring biblical guidelines, holding up their offerings, and not pleading, but declaring all the ways they expect God to cater to them as a result of their giving. The theology of, "I must increase" is peddled like a drug from the pulpits of American churches, and it is intoxicating.

We no longer live in fear of the authority of God or the unimaginable power of God. We no longer live with an awareness that God is selfish for His own glory, and declares in Isaiah 42:8 "my glory I give to no other." Instead, we have been conditioned over time to see God as a heavenly butler who is controlled by our demands, desires, and decrees. There is no acknowledgment of His glory and no concern for His infinite worth. God is a means to an end. Nothing more than a divine concierge who obliges our greed and selfishness. It is the pinnacle of biblical ignorance. It is verbal excrement from the mouths of false teachers. A destructive false gospel that has given birth to a self-centered, artificial Christianity that seeks self-promotion and personal satisfaction.

John 3:30 screams in the face of the prosperity gospel, "untrue." John 3:30 stands in the face of humanism and loudly cries, "no!" John the Baptist never said, "I must increase." He never said, "Jesus owes me a promotion." He never said, "I am the answer to my problems, I am the captain, I am in control." His cry, his consuming passion was, "I must decrease." If you listen closely, you can even hear the submission in his voice as he utters those three words. Nothing in his flesh would have ever wanted to make such a statement. Only the convicting power of the Holy Spirit could make humility a person's greatest ambition. Decreasing is so inconvenient. It's so much easier for us to devote our energy to increasing. Increasing feels better. The tangible rewards associated with increasing are physically gratifying, but the person who pursues a lifestyle of decreasing doesn't experience those same rewards. He or she knows there aren't going to be any immediate rewards. The person who battles his or her flesh for the purpose of decreasing has his or her full attention on the invisible, eternal rewards of heaven. He or she believes Romans 8:18, that any suffering that is endured on the Earth isn't worthy to even be compared to the glory that awaits a child of God in heaven.

John the Baptist had to have laid hold on living for heaven's sake. How else could he have possibly embraced the necessity of decreasing? John the Baptist had to have had an eternal perspective on life, and that Spirit-led eternal perspective demanded him to see decreasing as a "must." The original Greek communicates his resolve even more clearly. The implication is that John's declaration, "He must increase but I must decrease" was a mandate. The word "must" means to be ordained in the counsels of God. Decreasing wasn't John's idea, but rather, it was God's command. This means that while writing under the inspiration of the Holy Spirit, the Apostle John didn't offer this verse to us as a suggestion for our consideration, but with authority, he shared John the Baptist's confession with us for our conviction and implementation. He boldly communicated to everyone who would ever read John 3:30, personal conviction matters, and apart from conviction it is impossible to live your life for Jesus' perpetual increase.

Unfortunately, very few people in today's culture live directed by their personal convictions. Far more people live morally and spiritually fluid lives. Relativism rules the day as people attempt to build solid lives, families, and futures on quicksand. The idea that truth is subjective and absolutes are nonexistent is nothing short of dangerous. The majority of two generations are living with more commas and question marks than they are periods and exclamation points. That is why strong words like those found in John 3:30 are viewed as archaic and overbearing. It's fine as long as those words occupy space on a page in the Bible, but it's not fine for anyone to even suggest that those seven words should determine the way we live. However, that is exactly what John was saying. "He must—I must" or "Because He has to increase, I have to decrease." That was John's conviction, and I believe the Spirit inspired him to share it so that it could be ours as well.

Believing "He must increase, but I must decrease" doesn't mean you understand how you are supposed to live that out. Sure, personal humility requires living in total submission to Jesus. Sure, living in total submission to Jesus requires believing that He has full ownership of you. Sure, you will never embrace that lifestyle apart from Holy Spirit–initiated conviction, but decreasing is only one part of the verse. Which means it is possible for you to sink to the lowest depths of humility and still not fully experience John 3:30. Life can't fully be experienced apart from Jesus increasing through your life, but how is it possible for Jesus to increase? How can the one who declared in Matthew 28:18, "All authority in heaven and on earth has been given to me," increase? That is a great question because we know that He can't increase in His sinlessness according to 2 Corinthians 5:21 or in His deity according to John 1:1. He can't increase in His span according to Revelation 22:13 or even in His name's sake according to Philippians 2:9–11. So how is it possible for me to grasp Jesus increasing through my life? How can I adopt John's desire and promote the increase of Jesus? It seems impossible.

When John the Baptist made his confession, "He must increase, but I must decrease," his life and ministry were almost over. John had only been a forerunner to Jesus. Even the title indicated that his role was temporary and his assignment was specific. He was to herald the arrival of Jesus and then exit upon his arrival. John was a part of the once upon a time, but that was the extent of his part in the story. His honor would be pointing people to the "Lamb of God who would take away the sin of the world." Barnes wrote in his commentary, "No work is so honorable and joyful as the ministry of the gospel; none are so highly honored as those who are permitted to stand near the Son of God, lead perishing men to His cross."

That was John's ministry and message: look, there is Jesus, the hope of the world. Before the sound of the hammer ever echoed across Golgotha, before sinless blood ever covered a crown of thorns, and before Jesus was ever suspended between heaven and earth on the cross, John had the great honor of pointing people to the Lamb who would be slain. That was all there was for John, and yet if it increased the fame of Jesus, it was enough. His temporary life was to be lived for Jesus' eternal glory, and that was all that mattered.

Jesus increased through John the Baptist's life because he used his life to exalt Jesus. He was satisfied to see Jesus glorified. The way John the Apostle described that satisfaction in John 3:28–29 couldn't possibly be more beautiful. Even now as I read those verses, I can't stop laughing and crying as John the Baptist's heart is put on display through his words. In my mind's eye, I picture him sitting on the ground with a few of his devoted followers surrounding him. John had to have been fully aware that Jesus' public ministry erased the need for his message, "prepare the way of the Lord," and knowing that had to create a flood of emotions. Preaching the message of Jesus' arrival had been his life, and now that Jesus had arrived, would there be another assignment for him?

Everyone seems to struggle when their season of usefulness is coming to an end, and yet John's resolve to see Jesus glorified was so strong that he gathered his disciples around him and said,

> The bride was never mine to have. I was never
> supposed to stand by her side. The attention,
> affection, and adoration of the bride was never

intended for me. I am the friend who steps to
the side and gazes on the bride's love for her
bridegroom with complete satisfaction. Jesus
is heaven's bridegroom, He is greater than me,
and my life's joy has been telling people about
Him. (author's paraphrase)

I'm so thankful that John the Apostle's gospel includes
John the Baptist's entire conversation with his disciples,
because it's what John the Baptist said after John 3:30 that
revealed the depth of his love for Jesus. He could have
been bitter and said it wasn't fair, but he didn't. He could
have said, "I was supposed to be a part of the wedding.
What about my moment of recognition? What about my
life?"

Instead, John saw Jesus being adored and praised. He
saw Jesus' ministry beginning and his coming to an end,
and at that moment, he made one of the most amazing
personal statements in all of the Bible, "therefore this joy
of mine is now complete." He was saying, "it's been a joy
to serve the cause of Jesus Christ. It's been a joy to have
a small part in God's redemption story. It's been a joy to
make Jesus more visible."

How could he say that his joy was completed by seeing
Jesus exalted and embraced? How could he be content to
die in virtual obscurity while Jesus was being adored by
the masses? It was because he took joy in the fact that
the purpose of his life was to point people to Jesus, and
he had done that. John the Baptist had used the time he
had to exalt Jesus. He had used the breaths that he had to
exalt Jesus. He had made much of the identity of Jesus at

the expense of his own identity. That is how he had promoted the increase of Jesus.

Seeing John the Baptist's acceptance of his role in God's story convinces me that we are missing it. Our cultural norm of, "notice me," "like my selfie," "admire my exciting life" makes it almost impossible for us even to understand the concept of finding significance by embracing insignificance. There is even competition in the Christian world. Singers, speakers, pastors, and writers are all trying to be the center of attention. Pastors want to be in front of the camera, on the cover of Outreach magazine, number one on the church growth chart. Christian bands want to headline the biggest concerts, perform in the largest venues, and occupy the number one spot on the Contemporary Christian Music Chart.

Pride and self-aggrandizement is the vacuum that has sucked us into making much of ourselves at the expense of making much of Jesus. Sadly, we don't even see that we're missing it. We're missing out on what we were saved to do. Making much of ourselves is not the Christian life. Our joy is supposed to be found in using our lives to make much of Jesus. Our lives are meant to be lived for the increase of His glory. We know this, but we're not living this. We are aware that our moments in this life are limited and that we are one breath away from exiting the story. So, why aren't we more urgent about using our lives to increase Jesus' visibility in the world around us? How awesome would it be to exit the story completely filled with joy because you used your moments on the earth to impact the increase of Jesus' fame? You and I can know that joy if Jesus is bigger to us than we are to ourselves.

We can exit the story with contentment if we know that we have lived our lives in a way that made Jesus stick out.

PRAYER

God, I pray that You will stick out in every area of my life. I bring before You my pride and arrogance, and I pray that everything that resembles pride in me would bow in submission to your greatness. May I live in acknowledgment of Your preeminence to the extent that You are first and foremost in my life. Lord, I pray that I would never want You for what I can get from You, but that my desire would always be for You. I also pray that the Holy Spirit would enable me to embrace John 3:30 to the extent that it is a part of my daily life. Make it my desire to be constantly decreasing so that You will constantly be increasing, and may my greatest joy in life be to make You visible. In Jesus' name, Amen.

REFLECT

1. What would Colossians 1:18 look like as a lifestyle? How would it change the way you live?

2. How does it impact your view of salvation when you see God as rightful owner of all that you are, and all that you have, your present, and your future?

3. What changes would have to occur immediately in your daily life if you implemented John 3:30?

4. In John 3:28–29, John the Baptist let it be known that honoring Jesus completed his joy—what about Jesus completes your joy?

"If he have faith, the believer cannot be restrained. He betrays himself. He breaks out. He confesses and teaches this gospel to the people at the risk of life itself."

Martin Luther

CHAPTER 6

VISIBLE JESUS IS WHO WE ARE AND WHAT WE DO

We live in a culture that labels and categorizes everyone. Religious belief, political affiliation, sexual preference, income, and even the year of your birth gets you labeled and categorized in our current system. Everyone is expected to wear their label and stay within the designated parameters of their assigned category. That is what our world has come to. A place where people are obsessed with creating safe spaces and social constructs. A place where new categories are constantly introduced for yet another segment of our society. One major university has even created a category for students who need puppies and Play-Doh in order to feel calm and safe, which proves there is no end to the madness of labeling and categorizing. Unfortunately, Christians haven't been exempted from the insanity, and even we are now divided by various labels and categories. No longer is the term "Christian" enough. That's far too broad for a political party to target, so we are now placed in specific categories and identified by specific labels. We are called evangelicals or right-wing evangelicals. We are identified as conservatives, liberals, or moderates. We are contemporary or traditional, pro-life or pro-choice, white or African American....The categories literally go on and on. Those who drive the national narrative decide who we are and where we belong. In the end, people's views and opinions of us are determined by the category in which we are placed. That is our current reality, but it shouldn't be.

Christians in our nation and around the world should be greatly offended by the cultural labels that have been placed on us. We shouldn't be offended by the people who have labeled us, but we should be offended with ourselves for resembling their labels. We should be bothered by the fact that we are seen as nothing more than a political demographic or a religious group. It should bother us that we are marginalized and viewed as just another category in our culture's expansive filing cabinet, but it doesn't seem to bother us at all. We don't seem all that offended. Instead, we have compromised so much and capitulated so often that we now proudly wear the labels that have been assigned to us. We have succumbed to the pressure of our society more than we have surrendered to the conviction of God's word. It's obvious we have lost our way. We should see this for what it is: a trap. It is a cultural mission that has distracted us from successfully living into God's mission.

Jesus never told His disciples to dedicate their energy to a political party. He never told His followers to serve the cause of national interests. That is not our mission.

Waving political banners or organizing rallies or marches on the National Mall is not what we've been commissioned to do. We aren't Americans and then Christians. We are Christians who are living in America, but our location doesn't change our mission at all. Regardless of where we live, our mission is always the same. Making Jesus visible in every place is always our primary objective. We aren't the pawns of a political party or the servants of a national organization. That's not who we are. We are the people of God on a mission for God. No single nation or government has the authority to categorize us. Our identity as Christians is, and should always be, defined by God. He alone has the authority to declare who we are and demand what we should do. His word hasn't assigned us to specific categories, but His word has identified us as a people who live for the fame of His name. That is our mission, and who we are and what we do ultimately identifies us as followers of Jesus Christ.

In 1 Corinthians 12:27, we are described as "the body of Christ." That's who we are—that's who God says we are. It isn't a brand that makes us distinct in the religious marketplace, but it's an identity that defines the mission we are called to fulfill. The "body of Christ" is who we are and what we do. Look closely at the words "the body of Christ" and think about everything that description reveals about our identity and our mission. You should immediately notice how powerfully it communicates that Christianity is not about us; it's about Jesus. Our personal identities aren't seen in this description at all. We know we are one of the members of His body, but we aren't individually named. The description only refers to us as the "body of Christ." Our identities are omitted, and His identity is not. Multiplied millions of people fused together and known only as "the body." The greatest Bible teachers, missionaries, para-church ministry leaders, and evangelists, all nameless and encompassed by this description, "the body." Maybe it's God's way of reminding us that our mission to make Jesus visible is bigger than any one of us individually, and that our personal recognition and our name's sake fades into nothingness when we successfully function as the body of Christ.

Charles Hodge wrote, "The Church is everywhere represented as one. It is one body, one family, one fold, one kingdom. It is one because pervaded by one Spirit. We are all baptized into one Spirit so as to become says the apostle, one body." This means every individual who makes up the church is numbered among the church, and our own identities and local church names are lost in the vastness of the universal body of Christ. Who we are individually disappears as we move together in unity as one church to make Christ known.

Whether a Christian lives in the remotest part of Africa or a high-rise apartment in Manhattan, they are equally included in the body of Christ. They are also equally expected to live out the mission of Christ, and that mission is communicated by the words "the body of Christ." After all, that's what we are supposed to be, the body of Christ physically portraying Jesus on the earth in our everyday lives. The people we work with see Jesus in the workplace because we are there. The people we go to school with see Jesus in the school because we are there. The people we live with see Jesus in the home because we are there. Everywhere we are, Jesus should be seen because we are there. He is made visible to the people around us through us, but that can only happen if we live out His description of us, "the body of Christ." That means living out His identity and attributes in front of the world around us. Being who He was and doing what He did while He was in His body.

Living that out starts with a desire to please God. That's why Jesus said everything He said and did everything He did because He was completely submitted to the will of God. Don Landis wrote in an article for *Answers In Genesis*, "Christ's entire life and ministry were orchestrated by His Father, and Jesus was careful to carry out every detail according to the will of His Father." That was the kind of statement Jesus made in Hebrews 10:7 when He was talking about life in the body God had prepared for Him: "Behold I have come to do your will, O God," which means we can never live out an accurate portrayal of the life of Jesus if we are not fully surrendered to the will of God for our lives. That's where it starts—with the prayer, "God I want to do what pleases you, what glorifies you, and what fulfills your purpose for my life."

Jesus did that, and we can't look like Jesus at all until we do that. Everything that Jesus did proceeded from that desire to live in total submission to the will of God. He lived blameless because that was God's will. He fed the hungry, cared for the sick, and wept with those who were grieving because that was God's will. He communicated the truth of God's word and lived out the commandments of God's word because that was God's will. Word by word, action by action, deed by deed, Jesus lived a life shaped by and surrendered to the will of God even when that included refusing to defend Himself when He was falsely accused. Even when it included not retaliating when He was mocked and abused, and even when it included not resisting when He was nailed to a cross to pay for sins He hadn't committed. Being the body of Christ and not just being called the body of Christ requires abandoning our resistance to the will of God and embracing our responsibility to live out the will of God. Our example is Jesus, and He said in John 6:38, "For I have come down from heaven, not to do my own will, but the will of Him who sent me." His prayer has to be our prayer if we are truly going to be the body of Christ. We have to know that God doesn't have us on the earth for the purpose of living out our own will, but for the purpose of living out His will, and His will is for us to make Jesus visible in the world in the same way Jesus made Him visible in the world. We have to embrace that truth if we ever expect to function as the body of Christ in our everyday lives.

That is a spiritual explanation of Jesus' life in His body and a spiritual explanation of how Jesus lived a fully surrendered life, but what would that look like practically in our everyday lives? For me, that is made clear not only in the gospels, but also in Romans 12. In the gospels, we have the great privilege of hearing Jesus speak to His critics as well as to those who were being discipled by Him. We hear His conversations with rebellious sinners and religious sinners. We have the privilege of listening in on His conversation with an adulteress and His defense of a weeping prostitute. Having the opportunity to hear Jesus' human interactions is priceless. The things He said and how He said them are the examples we are to follow. Not that we walk around always repeating His exact words, but that we find ways to apply the principles and practices He demonstrated in our own conversations.

The four gospels not only allow us hear Jesus speak, but they also enable us to see Jesus live. In the gospels, we see what Jesus cared about and what He didn't seem to care about at all. Homes, clothes, food, and worldly power seemingly meant nothing to Him, and people, preaching, and performing God's will meant everything. The gospels give us an opportunity to see Jesus interact with children. They allow us to watch Him care for the hurting, the sick, and the rejected. They show Him being patient with His disciples and obedient to earthly authority. They allow us to look on as He refuses to give into temptation and watch as He experiences suffering. In those moments, Jesus was saying to every disciple, from every generation, I have set the perfect example, now "follow me." 1 Peter 2:21 includes the statement "follow in His steps," and that's what we learn to do as we observe Jesus through the gospels living in a human body.

However, the gospels aren't the only place in scripture that we find practical instructions for Christian living. In Romans 12, Paul's description of the marks of a true Christian couldn't possibly be more practical. They also couldn't be more important for the person who desires to live for Jesus. The very fact that this segment of scripture is referred to as the marks of a true Christian implies that these marks will exist in the person who is like Christ. That is literally what it means to be a Christian, to be like Christ, and just as it did in Jesus' life, it begins in our life with complete submission to God's will. Romans 12:1–2 says, "present your bodies as a living sacrifice, holy and acceptable to God, which is your spiritual worship. Do not be conformed to this world, but be transformed by the renewal of your mind, that by testing you may discern what is the will of God." It always starts with the will of God, and everything else always follows that point of total surrender, and since Jesus is the only one who successfully lived that life, He is the only one who can produce that life in us.

Remember, we are the body of Christ, and we know that Christ in His body lived as a sacrifice to God wholly fixed on carrying out the perfect will of God. Which means, since we are "in Christ," we should resemble Christ, and have a consuming passion for living as He lived, fully surrendered to God's will (Coll. 1:1–4). If that isn't our consuming passion, we will never bear in our bodies the marks of a true Christian as they are recorded in Romans 12:9–21:

> Let love be genuine. Abhor what is evil; hold fast to what is good. Love one another with brotherly affection. Outdo one another in showing honor. Do not be slothful in zeal, be fervent in spirit, serve the Lord. Rejoice in hope, be patient in tribulation, be constant in prayer. Contribute to the needs of the saints and seek to show hospitality. Bless those who persecute you; bless and do not curse them. Rejoice with those who rejoice, weep with those who weep. Live in harmony with one another. Do not be haughty, but associate with the lowly. Never be wise in your own sight. Repay no one evil for evil, but give thought to do what is honorable in the sight of all. If possible, so far as it depends on you, live peaceably with all. Beloved, never avenge yourselves, but leave

it to the wrath of God, for it is written, "Vengeance is mine, I will repay, says the Lord." To the contrary, "if your enemy is hungry, feed him; if he is thirsty, give him something to drink; for by so doing you will heap burning coals on his head." Do not be overcome by evil, but overcome evil with good.

These verses erase the excuse, "I just don't know what it means to live a Christian life." We can't read these verses and say we don't know. God couldn't be any more practical. Twenty-nine marks of an authentic Christian life—not twenty-nine steps to becoming a Christian; not in order to be, but because you are. In other words, living all of these out to the best of our ability will never make any one of us a Christian, but because we are Christians, we have a desire to live these out.

None of these marks come naturally. We are inclined to pride, vengeance, division, selfishness, and sin. That's why we have to have Jesus. We can't live out any of these marks on our own. We don't even have the power to live out the first one. We aren't capable of loving genuinely on our own, or in our own strength. We love conditionally; we love temporarily, but loving genuinely, without any hypocrisy, is not in us. If we move to the next mark, the answer is the same, and each one of us would have to confess, "I can't do that on my own." That is always the answer for every Christian attribute because we are incapable of living differently without Him.

We are so helpless we can't even make Him visible without His help. If it looks like the "body of Christ," then we are incapable of accomplishing it on our own, but the great news is, we are not on our own. We have experienced the power of the love of God, the power of the saving work of Jesus Christ, and the enabling power of the Holy Spirit. The result of that power is a Christian life that is not produced by us, but that is being produced in us.

Paul pointed this out in 1 Corinthians 15:10 by saying, "But by the grace of God I am what I am, and his grace toward me was not in vain. On the contrary, I worked harder than any of them, though it was not I, but the grace of God that is with me." This only makes sense to a believer. No one else would read this and say, "I get it." Paul said, I worked hard, but it wasn't me, it was the grace of God. If you had asked Paul the question, is living for the glory of God really difficult? The answer would have been yes! Could Paul have accomplished anything of eternal value in his own strength? The answer would be no! So that can only mean one thing: there was a power at work in him that was beyond him, that gave him the strength to make Jesus visible through his life and ministry.

For example, there are sixty-one nuclear power plants in the United States, and combined, they produce nearly 20 percent of America's electricity. Each day, millions of people enjoy the visible benefits of electricity in their homes, on their jobs, and throughout their communities because of those nuclear power plants. What those people don't see is power plant using nuclear fission to create steam that spins a turbine that in turn generates electricity. The air conditioning cooling, the lights illuminating, the television functioning, the computer operating, all of those are all the result of electricity, but electricity is not its own power source. The electricity is the product of

the nuclear fission producing steam and the steam spinning a turbine.

I'm confident that you are seeing my point, but let me
walk through it just in case. Anything and everything we
do for the glory of God is like that electricity; it's seen,
and it's experienced, but it is the result of the unseen,
inward work of the Holy Spirit's nuclear power spinning
a life-changing turbine inside of us. This means when
someone sees Christianity on display through us, it's
only electricity. There is a source of energy at work in us,
equipping us to live in a way that makes Jesus visible to
the people around us.

Philippians 2:12 charges us to work out our own salvation with fear and trembling, but then verse 13 follows
with these words: "for it is God who works in you, both
to will and to work for His good pleasure." Those words
assure us that God is invisibly working in us, and His invisible work produces our visible work. If God weren't
at work in us, there would be nothing for us to work
out. Only God can give us the strength to live for Jesus'
recognition.

Only God can strengthen us to live a Romans 12 life.
Not so that we can be noticed or praised, but so that we
can look like and live like the body of Christ. When He
loves genuinely through our bodies as He loved genuinely
in His own body according to 1 John 3:16, it gets Him noticed. When He causes us to abhor evil like He abhorred
the author of evil in Matthew 4:10, it causes people to
take notice of Him. When He sustains us so that we are
patient in tribulation like He was patient in tribulation
according to Hebrews 12:2, it directs people's attention to
Him. When He strengthens us to care for the needs of the

saints in the same way He cared those who were in need in Matthew 14:13–21, it puts Him on display.

Each time He enables us to do anything that couldn't possibly be the result of our own ability, it directs people's attention toward Him. That's what motivates me to pray after reading Romans 12, Lord please produce these marks in me so the people who encounter me will see more of you. That should always be our burning desire, that people would see the life that Jesus lived by seeing the life that we live. That can only happen if we live out our identity and our mission as the body of Christ.

When Jesus was on the earth, people looked to Him for hope. For years they had lived in the gloom of hopelessness, and they longed for a light to pierce the darkness. Every day was a struggle, and the more poverty and oppression demeaned them, the more they longed for hope. Each time another young Jewish girl was sexually abused by a Roman soldier or another Jewish son was forced into slavery, they longed for hope. When their crops were destroyed and their communities ravaged, they longed for hope. When their loved ones suffered from disease and their families ached because of distress, they longed for hope.

That's what they saw in Jesus: hope. To them, He was a physical representation of a miraculous hope. What else would drive a dying woman to press through a crowd, in spite of legal consequences, because she knew she had to touch the hem of His garment? What else would cause ten lepers to fall on their faces and instead of crying out, "unclean," cry out, "Jesus have pity on us?" What else would cause a concerned father to leave his sick daughter's bedside and walk the streets in search of Jesus? What other explanation is there for a desperate mother allowing herself to be likened to a dog begging for crumbs from its master's table? There was no reason for the drastic measures that people took to encounter Jesus other than that they really believed if they came to Jesus, they would find hope. That's what they were searching for then, and that is what the world is still searching for now: hope.

People really want to believe there is still hope in the world. We see people by the thousands plunge headlong into the political process every four years because they long for hope. Other people turn to addictions, or sexual indulgences, or life experiences, all because they are longing for hope. The pain of hopelessness hurts too much. Existing without a glimmer of hope is just too dark, and that's where countless millions of people feel like they are living every day. They want to hope, but they are convinced there is nothing true and authentic to hope for. They are searching through the endless calamities and constant failures of our natural world, and one person after another, one broken promise after another, and one disappointment after another leave them believing there is no hope.

We know that's the condition of the world around us, but do we ever stop and think about what an amazing opportunity that presents for us to be the body of Christ? Do we really understand that if we lived to make Jesus visible, people would rush to find hope in us like they rushed to find hope in Him? 1 Peter 3:15 says, "Always be prepared to make a defense [to give an answer] to anyone who asks you for a reason for the hope that is in you." The verse assumes that people will ask.

There is no "think about being prepared to give an answer just in case anyone happens to see some hope in you." The verse doesn't say that at all. The charge 1 Peter 3:15 gives us is, "be prepared to give a good answer because people are going to ask you about the hope that is in you." The Apostle Peter assumes that Christians are going to be so much more hopeful in the way they live that people are going to ask "why?" The other assumption that Peter makes is that Christians are going to make hope so obvious that people are going to see it. Why else would they ask us about our hope? They wouldn't. No one would ever ask anyone about a hope they didn't see.

So, the expectation is that we would never hide this wonderful hope we have in Jesus that transcends every earthly hardship. On the contrary, we look for opportunities to put our hope on display. When we are suffering, we are not without hope. When we are grieving, we are not without hope. When we are confused, we are not without hope. Regardless of the situation we're in or the circumstances we are under, we are not without hope.

A few days ago while watching the news, I saw a man named Jeremiah put his hope on display for everyone to see. He and his young son were walking through the floodwaters of hurricane Harvey when a news reporter approached him for an interview. The reporter asked where they were going. Jeremiah responded, "I don't know, we have nothing left, but God is good." The news reporter was noticeably shocked and asked Jeremiah, "you're thankful?" Jeremiah responded, "yes we are thankful, God is good." I was amazed by Jeremiah's spirit in that tragic moment and incredibly encouraged by his powerful display of hope. In an interview that only lasted for a few seconds, he communicated this message, that we have nothing, but our hope isn't in our things. We have no car, no home, no clothes, but our hope isn't in cars, clothes, and homes. We have no idea how we're going to make it, but regardless of the trial we are facing at this moment, God is good. That testimony set Jeremiah apart. While others were complaining, fussing, and demanding that something be done, Jeremiah was saying to the world, "our hope is in God."

That is the kind of hope that causes people to ask questions. "Why is he walking through the floodwaters of hurricane Harvey saying, God is good?" Why after losing everything would he still be saying, "God is good?" That is the kind of hope the world needs to see in us, and when they ask, Why are you hopeful? Our answer is, 1 Timothy 1:1, "because Jesus is our Hope." Yes, the political climate in our nation is troubling, but I'm hoping for the day when Jesus rules and reigns. Yes, I am surrounded by pain and death, but I'm hoping for the day when Jesus eliminates pain and death forever. Yes, there are times when I cry because of the sorrow or the discouragement that I'm feeling, but I'm hoping for the day when Jesus wipes all tears from my eyes.

That is how we put hope on display. We show the hopeless people around us that having Jesus means having hope in every situation. Jesus did that in His body when He talked to the disciples about His own death. He said to them in John 14:1, "Let not your hearts be troubled." Who says that in a conversation about their own death? The people hearing that had spent the last three years of their lives with Jesus. They had given up everything for Him. Everything they believed in was

132 • BRIAN EDWARDS

completely wrapped up in Him, and yet in the same conversation He told them about His death, He charged them not to let their hearts be troubled. He was able to include those contrasting statements in the same conversation because He was able to point the disciples to a greater hope. He was able to say, "I go to prepare a place for you, and if I go to prepare a place for you, I will come again and will take you to myself, that where I am you may be also."

This was Jesus' way of saying to the disciples, "you are not being left hopeless." In spite of the pain, there is hope. In spite of the confusion, there is hope, and the great news is, we still have that message. Jesus was the gospel in the flesh, and now as His body, we are to be the gospel in the flesh. As the body of Christ, we look at the cross and see the empty tomb. We look at the death and see the deliverance. We look at sin and rejoice in salvation. We are able to look out over our dark, devastated world, and say, "there is hope." There is a hope that exceeds every trial, tear, and turmoil. That is what the body of Christ represents. We are people of hope. Our hope has a name, and His name is Jesus, and just as people ran to Him to find hope, people should be running to us to find hope, but that can't happen if it goes unseen and unsaid. Like Jesus, we have to point the people we encounter to a greater hope. We have to let everyone know why we have hope in a hopeless world.

One of my family's favorite places to visit is the Portland Headlight in Cape Elizabeth, Maine, just outside of the city of Portland. It is so special to us that our oldest daughter, Kelsey, chose to have her wedding there. She couldn't think of a more beautiful place to celebrate her once-in-a-lifetime special day. As usual, the beauty of Fort Williams Park did not disappoint us. The beautiful green grass, the rocky coastline, the crashing waves, and the cirrus clouds decorating the light blue sky were all captivating, but as always, the lighthouse was the main attraction. People who had never enjoyed the views of that special place stood in awe as they admired the beauty of the lighthouse. After all, it is the most photographed lighthouse in the world for a reason. The website *Trip Advisor* refers to it as a "photographer's dream." However, the lighthouse wasn't built to be admired. It wasn't designed to be a tourist attraction. In 1791, it was constructed to guide ships safely into the Portland Harbor. It was built to be a beacon of hope to ships that were sailing in the darkness. It was also a beacon of hope for ships that were being raided during the American Civil War. History records that a ship's captain would hope to see the light piercing the darkness as soon as possible. That is why the headlight was built. It's location, design, and purpose were to give light to those who were in darkness.

When I stand at the Portland Headlight, I always see more than a beautiful place—I see a spiritual reminder. A reminder that every Christian who makes up the body of Christ should be like a lighthouse. We should all be beacons shining the light of Jesus Christ into the dark world around us. That is our purpose. Our light says to the world around us, "there is hope." The people who encounter us shouldn't be shipwrecked because of a lack of light. They shouldn't have to try to feel their way through the darkness hoping to find help while we sit idly by. The light that is shining through us should say to them, "There is safety in this direction, there is protection in this direction, there is help in this direction, there is hope if you will just sail toward Jesus." That's what Jesus did in His body. In John 8:12 He said, "I am the light of the world. Whoever follows me will never walk in darkness, but will have the light of life," and that's what Jesus will do in our body when we live as the body of Christ. In 1 Peter 2:9 He calls us a "chosen people...who declare the praises of Him who called us out of darkness into His wonderful light." So when was the last time someone heard you share the story of that moment when Jesus guided you out of the darkness into the light? When was the last time you were a lighthouse that guided someone safely into the port of salvation? When was the last time you made Jesus visible by allowing Him to do in your body what He did in His body? When was the last time you were recognized as the body of Christ? If we fail to shine the light of Jesus across our dark world, how are people going to know that there is hope?

Try to imagine the virgin birth being kept a secret. The story of the infinite God becoming finite man being kept hush-hush. Try to imagine no one ever sharing the news that the Savior of the world had been born in Bethlehem. Stop and think what the world would be like if no one knew that Jesus ever lived. What would the world be like if no one knew that Jesus lived the sinless life they could never live? What if no one knew that He died the sacrificial death that they should have died? What if no one knew that He rose again on the third day to secure salvation and eternal life for them? Imagine how dark the world would be without the message of Jesus. The orphanages, hospitals, universities, and care centers that exist because of His story would all disappear. The millions of hungry people around the world who have been fed in His name would all be left hopeless and hungry. The homeless men and women who have been given a hot meal and a warm bed on a cold winter's night by someone who loved Jesus would be left overlooked, empty, and cold. There would be no laughter. There would be no true love. There would be no hope of an eternity in heaven. The story of a world without Jesus would be a sad story. The thought of the gospel of Jesus never being shared is a dark, devastating thought. The idea of Jesus' disciples keeping His life, death, and resurrection a secret is frightening. If they hadn't been willing to share the story of Jesus at the expense of their own lives, just think about hopeless the world would be.

That's why it should alarm us to think about what the world is going to look like for future generations, if our generation of Christians fail to make Jesus visible. My heart aches to even think about a world with fewer people making Jesus known. We can't allow that to happen. We have to rise up and live as the body of Christ with an all-consuming passion to make Jesus known. There needs to be an awakening in us that drives us to live every moment of every day looking for opportunities to put Jesus on display. Visible Jesus has to be more than a dream, it has to be more than an idea, it has to be more than a concept—it has to be an uprising in the church that drives us to make Jesus known through our lives. D.L. Moody said, "our greatest fear in life should not be of failure, but of succeeding at things in life that don't really matter." If we live and die without making Jesus visible, we have failed to accomplish the only thing in life that really matters at all. I pray with all of my heart that each one of us would live with a greater passion than ever before to show the glory and the splendor of Jesus to the world around us. The only way they will ever see Him is if they see Him in us.

PRAYER

God, I pray that I will daily submit my body as a living sacrifice to you. That I would do in life, what Jesus did in death, which is to surrender to Your will completely. God, I pray that the more I surrender to you, the more the marks of true Christianity will be seen in my life, and the more those marks are seen in my life, the more Jesus will be seen through my life. God, may the Holy Spirit work powerfully in my life to produce a greater faith in me regarding the hope I have in You. Make me a lighthouse that directs people safely into the harbor of salvation. Strengthen me to live as Your body in Your absence. I want to be the body of Christ so that You will be visible to others through me regarding the hope I have in You. Make me a lighthouse that directs people safely into the harbor of salvation. Strengthen me to live as Your body in Your absence. I want to be the body of Christ so that You will be visible to others through me.

REFLECT

1. List some of the ways you see the culture defining Christianity, and how cultural Christianity looks different than Biblical Christianity:

2. If you journaled Christian behaviors and characteristics as seen in the Bible, what would you believe about being a Christian, and what would you believe about Christian behavior ?

3. Read Romans 12:9–21 and honestly identify which marks need to be produced or strengthened by the Holy Spirit in you?

4. What is the difference between striving to be a successful Christian, and yielding to be a surrendered Christian?

5. Can you identify one person you know who is desperate for hope? If you have someone in mind, call them, visit them, or send them a card of encouragement as soon as possible and be visible Jesus to them.

6. How are you planning to take this book from print to practice? List several ways you believe you can make Jesus visible to the people around you. How are you going to change your part of the world by making Jesus visible?

Challenge: Don't Just Read This, Live This

I have a deep concern that many of you, who have just read *Visible Jesus* will respond by agreeing with the content intellectually, but that is where it will stop.

I am also concerned that others of you will plan to make Jesus visible when the perfect opportunity presents itself. You know, if and when you are ever in a situation, and the planets align, and the weather is favorable, you will do what you can to live into a visible Jesus moment.

Neither of those responses mean that you are infected with apathy, or rebelliously unwilling, but it could be that in your mind making Jesus visible is beyond you. Maybe you think this is something complicated, and it should be lived out by "better Christians" who know, and understand more.

If that is what you are thinking, then your thinking is wrong. Making Jesus visible could be as simple as volunteering at an organization in your community that is outwardly loving people in Jesus' name, or preparing meals with a purpose, or hosting a backyard Vacation Bible School for children in your neighborhood, or creating a missions calendar for your family with local projects for elderly people, or it could be volunteering at your local church, or visiting a hospital waiting room and praying a simple prayer of encouragement with an anxious family.

The ways you can personally make Jesus visible are almost endless. You don't have to be a great speaker, or a bible scholar—you only have to be a follower of Jesus who is willing to let the faith you have in Jesus show. Making Jesus visible is making Jesus known. He is the gospel, and if we share Him, lives will be changed.

In Matthew 10:42, Jesus encouraged the simple gesture of giving someone a drink of cold water in His name. Hebrews 6:10 gives the promise, "God is not unjust so as to overlook your work and the love that you have shown for His name in serving the saints."

Visible Jesus is simple. It's showing His name and His identity by any and every means possible. So here is my challenge to you: start today. Don't wait! Right now, start to imagine all of the ways you can make Jesus visible by using the energy, opportunities, and gifts you have. James 1:22 says it best: "be doers of the word, and not hearers only." Or to make it really simple, "Don't just read and listen, but do what you've read and heard." Take this challenge and be the body of Christ wherever you are, and if enough of us do that, together, we can make Jesus visible.

Scripture References

Matthew 7:3,4,5
Acts 4:20
2 Corinthians 12:9
Luke 2:43
Matthew 4:20
John 21:15
James 1:14
Ruth 1:16,17
Matthew 4:18
Philippians 3:10
Acts 9:3-7
Philippians 3:8
Ephesians 2:10
Genesis 1:3
John 3:16
2 Corinthians 6:15
Titus 2:14
2 Peter 1:5,6,7,8
Proverbs 3:6
Galatians 6:10
Acts 8:26–39
Philippians 2:13
Matthew 5:14,15
Ephesians 5:8

Matthew 10:33
1 John 1:1,2,3,4,5,6,7
James 2:19
2 Corinthians 6:2
Matthew 28:20
John 14:15
Matthew 28:19
Luke 6:45
Luke 12:34
Revelation 3:20
Luke 2:7
1 John 3:1
1 John 4:19
Ephesians 2:8,9
Revelation 5:9
Revelation 5:12
2 Corinthians 5:17,18,19
2 Corinthians 5:20,21
1 John 4:18
2 Corinthians 4:3
Mark 6:34
John 1:12
2 Thessalonians 1:8,9,10
Colossians 1:18
1 Corinthians 6:20
1 Peter 1:18,19
John 3:30
Daniel 1 & 2
Isaiah 42:8
John 1:1
Revelation 22:13
Philippians 2:9,10,11

John 3:28-29
Galatians 6:10
Acts 8:26-39
1 Corinthians 12:27
Hebrews 10:7
John 6:38
1 Peter 2:21
Colossians 1:1,2,3,4
Romans 12:9–21
1 Corinthians 15:10
Philippians 2:12,13
1 John 3:16
Matthew 4:10
Hebrews 12:2
Matthew 14:13–21
1 Peter 3:15
1 Timothy 1:1
John 14:1
John 8:12
1 Peter 2:9
Acts 11:20,21,23,26
Matthew 10:42
Hebrews 6:10
James 1:22

Notes

A Call To Resurgence, Mark Driscoll, Tyndale House Publishers Inc, Carol Stream, Illinois, 2013.

The Disappearance of God, R. Albert Mohler Jr., Multnomah Books, Sisters, Oregon, 2009.

"Pulpit Commentary," Joseph Exell, H.D.M. Spence studylight.org.

Our Daily Bread, "Walking In His Dust," Anne Cetas, Grand Rapids, Michigan, September 2005.

Rufus Stone quote, Andy Lane, Fire Storm (Young Sherlock Holmes #4) goodreads.com.

Seeing And Savoring Jesus Christ, John Piper, Crossway Books, Wheaton, Illinois, June 14, 2004.

Lectures On The Acts Of The Apostles, John Dick, Forgotten Books, London, UK, May 4, 2017.

The Acts Of The Apostles, G. Campbell Morgan, New York: Fleming H. Revell Company, 1924.

Jesus Continued, J.D. Greear, Zondervan, Grand Rapids, Michigan, November 4, 2014.

Matthew Henry's Commentary Volume VI, Matthew Henry, Fleming H. Revell Company, 1662–1714.

Wiersbe Bible Commentary, Warren Wiersbe, David C. Cook, Colorado Springs, Colorado, November 1, 2007.

Power Filled Living, R.A. Torrey, Whitaker House, New Kensington, Pennsylvania, July 1, 1999.

The Normal Christian Life, Watchmen Née, Tyndale House, Carol Stream, Illinois, 1977.

Dietrich Bonhoeffer, Jonathan Parnell, *Desiring God*, Minneapolis, Minnesota, January 29, 2012.

Gypsy Smith, Bible Gateway Blog, Johnathan Peterson, July 28, 2014

Johann Bengel, *Gnomon of the New Testament*, 1860–1866, Logos Research Systems Inc., Bellingham, Washington.

Charles Hodge *Commentary Collection*, Charles Hodge, Logos Research Systems Inc., Bellingham, Washington.

Don Landis, President of Jackson Hole Bible College, Jackson Hole, Wyoming, Answers In Genesis Blog.

D.L. Moody, *Stand Strong In Your Faith*, Alex McFarland, Jason Jimenez, BroadStreet Publishing Group LLC, Savage, Minnesota, June 1, 2017.

Explore The Book, J. Sidlow Baxter, Zondervan Publishing House, Grand Rapids, Michigan, 1960.

The Purpose Driven Life, Rick Warren, Zondervan Publishing House, Grand Rapids, Michigan, 2002.